# FOR
# REAL
# BLOKES
## ONLY

The ultimate cookbook for men

# Contents

# Introduction

As much as you may enjoy dishes like spaghetti and curry, do you also relish delicious, traditional home cooking? Would you like to learn to cook some of these dishes yourself? If so, this is the perfect book for you! With recipes ranging from quick and easy everyday meals and hearty classics to elegant yet foolproof dishes which are guaranteed to impress, this cookbook contains all that is needed to delight a real man's stomach and set his heart beating faster!

No one can be an expert at everything, so for those of you who may be relatively new to cooking, we have included explanations of some of the basic terms and techniques you may find in the recipes as well as some useful tips and tricks which will hopefully prevent things going wrong as your chosen dish makes its way from the shopping basket and onto the dinner plate.

And finally, a word on the subject of portions: the estimated number of portions given for each recipe is based on average amounts; depending on the occasion and size of appetite, the portions will be enough for 2–4 people.

Enjoy!!

## COOKING METHODS AND TECHNIQUES

### Au gratin
This cooking term means baking a dish until the topping, usually breadcrumbs or cheese, is golden brown and is slightly crusty. Nearly all ingredients are suitable for baking in the oven this way or under a grill.

### Bain-marie
A bain-marie is used to warm, melt or cook delicate ingredients in an open or closed container, suspended over hot or boiling water. A bain-marie is suitable for making custards, egg cream, chocolate and sauces. To prepare a bain-marie, heat water in a large saucepan to about 80 °C, then stand a bowl containing the cream or other ingredient in the water and keep stirring constantly.

### Blanching
Blanching means briefly cooking ingredients, usually vegetables, in boiling water. The vegetables are plunged into boiling, salted water, cooked briefly, then removed with a slotted spoon and chilled under running, cold water. This technique is particularly suitable for vegetables which do not require much cooking time (such as spinach, broccoli or fine green beans).

### Boiling (simmering)
Boiling involves cooking food in plenty of liquid at boiling temperature (100 °C).

### Braising
Braising is a cooking method whereby the meat or vegetables are first browned, then cooked in a covered pot with the addition of a small amount of water over a low heat at approx. 100 °C. An important point to remember when braising is that the base of the pot must be covered with liquid at all times and the lid must fit snugly.

### Deep-frying
This technique involves cooking in plenty of fat at temperatures from 180–200 °C. This can be carried out in an ordinary saucepan or in a deep-fat fryer. Pieces of meat, poultry or fish, breaded or encased in pastry, as well as potatoes, vegetables or doughnut-style pastries, are well suited to this cooking method. Fats suitable for this purpose include palm oil, coconut oil or refined olive oil.

### Deglazing
When meat or vegetables have been browned in a pan, a deposit forms and sticks to the bottom of the pan. A liquid, such as stock or wine, is added which acts as a solvent and dissolves the brown deposits on the bottom of the pan so they can be used as the base for a sauce.

### Draining
Ingredients which have been cooked in liquid (usually vegetables, potatoes or pasta) are strained through a sieve or colander to drain off the cooking liquid.

### Frying versus roasting
Smaller, flat types of food such as patties, thin cuts of meat, vegetables and sausages are best fried or sautéed in a frying pan on the hob. Some ingredients may

also be suitable for quick-frying. The oven is generally more suitable for roasting larger items such as meat roasts, whole fish and poultry, usually at temperatures between 160 and 250 °C.

## Grilling

Grilling involves cooking food under strong, radiated heat. Meat, fish and poultry, as well as fruit and vegetables, can all be cooked using this method. A charcoal grill, a worktop grill, a contact grill or an oven grill can all be used to grill food in this way.

## Low-heat cooking

This method is mainly used by professional cooks and is a cooking method guaranteed to produce extra-tender meat. The meat is first seared briefly over a high heat to seal in the juices, then cooked for several hours in the oven at a temperature between 80 and 100 °C.

## Marinating

Marinating means leaving ingredients – such as meat, poultry, fish or vegetables – to stand for several hours or days in an aromatic mixture of oil, wine or vinegar, containing herbs and spices, in order to intensify their flavour and increase tenderness.

## Poaching

Poaching involves cooking an ingredient in liquid at a temperature below boiling point. This cooking method is particularly suitable for tender cuts of meat, fish, poultry, fruit, dumplings and eggs.

## Puréeing

This means blending what are – for the most part – cooked ingredients into a smooth paste with the aid of a hand-held blender or using a sieve, pestle and mortar, etc. The best-known example in this respect is probably potato purée, although potatoes should actually never be puréed but only ever mashed.

## Reducing

Reducing means cooking liquids, such as stock, meat juices, sauces or cream, quite briskly to reduce the amount of liquid, thereby thickening the consistency and intensifying the flavour.

## Roasting

Ingredients such as coffee beans, nuts, almonds or chestnuts are roasted to intensify their aromatic qualities. They can be roasted in an oven or toasted in a frying pan, always without the addition of fat or liquid.

## "Shocking"

This means "shocking" the vegetables by pouring cold water over them or dipping them in ice water after blanching to halt the cooking process and retain colour and nutrients.

## Steaming

Steaming is a technique whereby ingredients are cooked in a combination of steam and air at a temperature around 100 °C. This gentle cooking method minimises the loss of any minerals or vitamins. With the exception of pulses, white, red and green cabbage or asparagus, any food is suitable for steam-cooking. Food can be steamed in any ordinary saucepan fitted with a sieve insert, or in a steaming basket, steamer pan or steam oven.

## Stewing

Stewing means cooking ingredients in their own juice with the addition of a little fat and liquid in a covered pot or in aluminium foil at a temperature of 100 °C. This cooking technique is ideal for foods such as vegetables, fish, meat and fruit, which have a high water content.

## Stir-frying

This is a quick, healthy cooking method whereby the ingredients are cut into small pieces, then fried quickly in a wok or high-sided frying pan containing a small amount of fat whilst constantly stirring the ingredients or shaking the wok to prevent sticking.

## Straining or sieving

This technique involves straining the respective ingredient or liquid through a sieve to remove any solid bits, e.g. from fruit, jams or sauces.

## TIPS & TRICKS

### Cleaning, washing and peeling fruit and vegetables

- Whenever possible, wash the fruit and vegetables whole to minimise the loss of nutrients.
- Wash thoroughly, ideally in cold water, but as quickly as possible.
- Remove any tough parts of the fruit or vegetable or any bits which have gone bad or are wilted.
- Remove any inedible or hard parts of skin but peel as thinly as possible as the most valuable substances tend to be found directly under the outer layer.
- Peeled ingredients, especially fruit, should be used straight away as oxygen can cause discolouration and loss of vitamins. Alternatively, sprinkle with lemon juice and store in the fridge wrapped in cling film.
- It is best just to wipe mushrooms clean. Either avoid washing them at all or, at best, only briefly to prevent them absorbing water.

### Skinning tomatoes

- Cut a cross in the surface of the tomato.
- Plunge the tomatoes in boiling water for approx. 10 seconds, then lift them out of the water and shock them in ice-cold water.
- Peel off the skin using a vegetable knife and cut out the core.

### Cooking pasta *al dente*

- Bring 1 litre of water per 100 g of pasta to a boil in a large saucepan. The pan should only be three-quarters full (do not pour oil into the cooking water or the sauce will slide off the pasta later). Tip the pasta into the boiling water and stir well, making sure none is sticking to the bottom of the pan. Now – and not before – add a little salt, so that the water will be quicker to boil again. This is important as the pasta should cook rather than swell.
- To ensure the pasta does not become overcooked, test a piece after three-quarters of the recommended cooking time. If it is still too hard and floury, try again after a further minute. Continue doing so until the pasta is velvety but still firm (*al dente*) to the bite.
- Reserve some of the water drained off the pasta; it will help make the sauce creamier and the starch it contains will ensure that the sauce sticks to the pasta properly. Remember, too, that the pasta will continue to cook briefly after being drained, so mix it with the sauce and serve immediately. You should only shock pasta in cold water if you plan to turn it into a salad.

### Storing

- Fresh garlic cloves can be stored for a long time if placed in neutral oil and kept in the fridge. After a while, the oil absorbs the flavour of the garlic and can be used for seasoning.
- Raw meat should not be stored on a wooden board. The wood draws the juice out of the meat and dries it out.
- Fresh ginger can be stored for many months if it is peeled and conserved in dry sherry.
- Parsley stays fresh longest if wrapped in aluminium foil and stored in the fridge.

### Safety in the kitchen

- Place a damp cloth or kitchen towel under the chopping board to prevent it slipping.
- Avoid storing knives any old how in the cutlery drawer – make sure they lie flat and clearly visible in a tidy drawer. The best way to store knives is in a knife block.
- Make sure you do not leave the handles of pots and pans sticking out from the hob. They can easily get knocked or caught on clothing and lead to scaldings.

### Food hygiene

- Bacteria are not only a threat to raw fish, raw meat and dairy products but also to many cooked foods as well, especially those with a high starch content such as rice, pasta and beans. The simplest way to protect food from airborne bacteria is to make sure the food is covered.
- Bacteria need warmth to reproduce so always try and keep fish and meat in a cool place.

## This and that

- A quick way to pit olives is to lay the olives on a work surface and roll a rolling-pin over them a few times. This will make it much easier to extract the stones.
- Hard, dry bread need not be thrown away. Wrap it in a damp cloth, then, after a while, bake it in the oven for 30 minutes and you will find it is soft and fresh again.
- Do not prod meat with a fork or cut into with a knife during cooking or the juices will run out, leaving the meat dry.
- Breadcrumbed fish or meat should be cooked immediately as the coating will otherwise go soggy. Do not begin to coat the fish or meat in flour, eggs and breacrumbs until the fat is already sizzling in the frying pan.
- Leeks often have sand and grit between the layers. Slide a knife along the whole length of the leek starting at the green end without cutting all the way through. Then rinse thoroughly in running water.
- Whole spices, such as cloves, peppercorns or bay leaves, which are not meant to be eaten, can be cooked in a tea net or a small cloth pouch. This will save having to fish the individual spices out afterwards.
- Do not put the topping on a pizza until just before you are ready to bake it otherwise the pizza dough will go soggy.
- Frying large quantities of meat patties in a frying pan is very time-consuming and will fill your kitchen with a strong smell of frying. It is better to use an oven. Place the patties on a greased baking sheet and cook at 200 °C.
- Do not season meat with salt until just before use otherwise the salt will dry out the meat. Do not salt small chunks of meat, e.g. for goulash, until halfway through the cooking time.
- Salad leaves should not be wet when the dressing is poured over them or this will make it bland and watery and prevent it coating the leaves effectively. Salad leaves should always be dried in a salad spinner or in a tea towel. Place the salad on a tea towel, hold the four corners together and swing it around a few times.
- You can avoid unpleasant fish smells on your hands and kitchen equipment by wetting your hands before touching the fish, wiping kitchen utensils with paper before rinsing them in cold water and only then washing them in hot water using a detergent.
- Lettuce leaves will stay fresh longer if wrapped in kitchen towel and stored in a plastic bag or airtight container in the vegetable drawer of the fridge.
- Brushing meat with a little oil before grilling will make it juicier as the oil immediately seals the pores and prevents any juice from escaping. Depending on which type of oil you use, it can also be used as a seasoning.
- Pepper tastes best if freshly ground. It is well worth investing in a small pepper mill!
- Only use pre-packed, grated cheese as a very last resort –

freshly grated cheese tastes so much better!
- Before slicing, meat should be left to stand for 10 minutes after cooking. Otherwise, the juices will escape and the meat will not be as juicy.
- Salad dressing can be prepared well in advance. It can be kept for up to a week in the fridge if stored in a jar with a screw-top lid.
- If a dish is too hot and spicy, the flavour can be made a bit milder either by the addition of cream, yoghurt or coconut milk (in the case of Asian dishes) or by adding a whole or grated potato to the cookpot.

# Everyday meals

# Scrambled eggs and smoked salmon

Preparation time **approx. 15 minutes**

Quick and easy | per portion **approx. 282 kcal/1181 kJ, 7 g P, 11 g F, 33 g CH**

## SERVES 4

8 eggs
2 tbsp soy sauce
salt
cayenne pepper
2 tbsp freshly chopped dill
3 spring onions
200 g smoked salmon
3 tbsp oil
coriander leaves, to garnish

**1** Beat the eggs with the soy sauce, a little salt, cayenne pepper and the freshly chopped dill. Clean, wash and dry the spring onion, then slice into rings. Cut the smoked salmon into strips.

**2** Heat the oil in a frying pan and gently sauté the spring onions. Add the beaten eggs and strips of salmon and cook until the egg mixture thickens and is lightly set.

**3** Serve the scrambled egg garnished with coriander leaves. Serve with fresh wholemeal bread and butter.

Quick to make

# TIP!!

Toast the bread first, then spread with the scrambled egg and bacon mixture and serve with pickled gherkins.

# Scrambled eggs and bacon

Preparation time **approx. 20 minutes**

Quick and easy | per portion approx. 166 kcal/700 kJ, 12 g P, 10 g F, 8 g CH

## SERVES 4

100 g bacon
2 onions
440 ml milk
2 eggs
1 tbsp marjoram
1 tbsp flour
salt
pepper

**1** Dice the bacon. Peel and finely dice the onions. Sweat the bacon in a hot frying pan until the juices begin to run, then fry the onions until translucent.

**2** Lightly beat the milk, eggs, marjoram and flour together, and season with salt and pepper. Blend the mixture with the bacon in the frying pan. Cook until the eggs are beginning to set, then stir again and make sure the eggs stay a little bit runny. Serve the dish with farmhouse bread whilst still warm.

# Peppered gherkin breakfast

Preparation time approx. 30 minutes | plus infusion time approx. 30 minutes | ready in approx. 1 hour
Moderate | per portion approx. 432 kcal/1808 kJ, 22 g P, 36 g F, 6 g CH

## SERVES 4

8 large pickled gherkins
pepper
200 g ham sausage
200 g radish
3 eggs
300 g Camembert
6 tbsp mayonnaise
salt
1 dash of vinegar

**1** Slice the gherkins in half lengthways, scoop out the flesh, scraping away the seeds. Sprinkle the gherkins all over with pepper. Set the gherkin flesh aside.

**2** Cut the ham sausage into very small pieces; trim and finely dice the radish. Hard-boil, then dice, the eggs. Finely chop the scooped-out gherkin flesh. Dice the Camembert.

**3** Mix the gherkin, sausage, eggs, radish, mayonnaise, pepper, salt and a dash of vinegar together into a substantial spread, then stir in the diced Camembert.

**4** Leave the mixture to stand for approx. 30 minutes, then spoon it back into the gherkin shells. Serve with fresh bread.

Tasty in the evening too •••

# Eggs in mustard sauce

Preparation time **approx. 35 minutes**

Quick and easy | per portion **approx. 463 kcal/1943 kJ, 18 g P, 40 g F, 8 g CH**

## SERVES 4

8 eggs
2 onions
5 tbsp butter
3 tbsp flour
250 ml vegetable stock
200 ml cream
2 tbsp hot mustard
salt
pepper
2 tbsp freshly chopped parsley

**1** Hard-boil the eggs, then shock in cold water. Peel and finely chop the onions. Melt the butter in a saucepan and sweat the onions until softened. Stir in the flour and sauté for a few minutes. Add the stock and cream to the saucepan, then bring all the ingredients to a boil and allow the sauce to thicken, stirring constantly.

**2** Blend the mustard into the sauce and season with salt and pepper. Shell the eggs and cut them in half. Add the eggs to the sauce and let them absorb the flavours for a few minutes.

**3** Serve the eggs in mustard sauce and sprinkled with parsley. A green salad makes an excellent accompaniment to this dish.

# Farmhouse breakfast

Preparation time **approx. 30 minutes** | plus cooking time **approx. 20 minutes** | ready in **approx. 50 minutes**

**Moderate** | per portion **approx. 302 kcal/1268 kJ, 14 g P, 13 g F, 29 g CH**

## SERVES 4

750 g potatoes
2 tbsp butter
30 g bacon
salt
pepper
1 onion
125 g ham, cooked or raw
4 eggs
1 egg yolk
2 tbsp milk
1 tbsp freshly chopped chives
4 pickled gherkins

**1** Thoroughly brush the potatoes clean, then cook for about 20 minutes in boiling water. Drain off the water and leave to cool slightly, then peel and slice the potatoes.

**2** Melt the butter in a frying pan. Dice the bacon and fry gently in the butter until the fat begins to run. Sauté the sliced potatoes in the fat, turning frequently, until golden brown. Season with salt and pepper.

**3** Peel and dice the onions, and fry them along with the potatoes. Dice the ham and add to the fried potato mixture.

**4** Lightly beat the eggs, egg yolk and milk. Season the mixture, then pour over the potatoes. Cook over a gentle heat until the eggs are set. Sprinkle with chopped chives and serve each portion with a sliced gherkin.

## TIP !!

Where possible, always cook potatoes in their skins as this prevents the loss of important vitamins and minerals. Once cooked, remove as thin a layer of peel as possible since the most valuable nutrients are found just under the skin.

## TIP !!

To make an authentic American hot dog, leave off the cheese.

# Hot dogs

Preparation time **approx. 30 minutes**

Moderate | per portion approx. 209 kcal/876 kJ, 10 g P, 7 g F, 26 g CH

## SERVES 4

100 g mixed pickles
½ red onion
1 tomato
½ bunch chervil
4 hot dog sausages or
   frankfurters
4 hot dog rolls
8 slices of cheese
ketchup and mustard, to taste

**1** Drain and finely chop the mixed pickles. Peel and finely dice the onions. Wash the tomato, remove the stalk, then dice. Wash the chervil, shake dry and chop well. Mix all these ingredients with the mixed pickles.

**2** Cook the hot dogs under the grill or heat in hot water. Cut the rolls almost in half lengthways. Place 1 hot dog and 2 slices of cheese in each roll, then melt under the grill.

**3** Spread the pickle mixture over the cheese, sandwich the two halves of the roll together and serve the hot dogs with ketchup and mustard.

# Chicken wings with Cheese dip

Preparation time **approx. 20 minutes** | plus marinating time **approx. 1 hour** | plus grilling time **approx. 20 minutes**
ready in **approx. 1 hour 40 minutes**
Moderate | per portion approx. 828 kcal/3475 kJ, 49 g P, 69 g F, 4 g CH

## SERVES 4

1 kg chicken wings
3 tbsp butter
1 tsp paprika powder
1 tbsp each of hot pepper sauce
  and lemon juice
1 garlic clove
100 g blue cheese
50 g crème fraîche
50 g mayonnaise
150 g natural yoghurt
1 tbsp lemon juice
pepper
sugar

**1** Wash the chicken wings, pat dry then cut through the joint. To make the marinade, melt the butter and mix in the paprika powder, hot pepper sauce and lemon juice.

**2** Mix the marinade and the chicken wings together in a bowl and leave to stand for at least 1 hour. Then place the chicken wings under the grill and cook until nice and crisp, turning occasionally. This will take about 20 minutes.

**3** To make the dip, peel and finely chop the garlic. Mash the cheese with a fork and mix with the rest of the ingredients. Season with pepper and a pinch of sugar. Serve the chicken wings with the dip.

# Bacon pancakes with lamb's lettuce

Preparation time approx. 40 minutes

Moderate | per portion approx. 522 kcal/2192 kJ, 33 g P, 25 g F, 39 g CH

## SERVES 4

8 eggs
200 g flour
200 ml milk
mineral water
salt
pepper
250 g streaky bacon
4 tbsp clarified butter
1 ½ tsp mustard
3 tbsp white wine vinegar
4–5 tbsp sunflower oil
pinch of sugar
200 g lamb's lettuce

**1** Separate the eggs. Mix the egg yolks with the flour and milk and just enough mineral water to make a fairly liquid batter. Whisk the egg whites until stiff and add to the batter a little at a time. Season with salt and pepper.

**2** Dice the bacon into small pieces and fry in a frying pan until the fat begins to run. Reserving 1 tablespoon of bacon and the fat, mix the rest of the bacon into the batter. Heat 1 tablespoon of clarified butter at a time in a frying pan and make 4 pancakes, one after the other, transferring them to a warm oven heated to approx. 60 °C as each one is cooked.

**3** Combine the mustard, vinegar, salt, pepper, bacon fat, sunflower oil and sugar to make a dressing. Clean and wash the lamb's lettuce, then shake dry. Transfer to a bowl and drizzle the dressing over the top. Sprinkle the remaining bacon over the salad and serve as an accompaniment to the bacon pancakes.

## TIP!!

Lamb's lettuce often contains a good deal of grit so it needs to be washed very thoroughly.

Hot and crisp

# Potato rösti cakes

Preparation time **approx. 35 minutes**

Quick and easy | per portion approx. 243 kcal/1014 kJ, 7 g P, 7 g F, 38 g CH

## SERVES 4

1 kg potatoes
2 onions
2 eggs
salt
pepper
4–5 tbsp oil, for frying

**1** Wash, peel and grate the raw potatoes into a bowl. Peel and grate the onions and add to the potato. Add the eggs to the potato and onion mixture and mix all the ingredients into a smooth dough. Season to taste with salt and pepper.

**2** Heat the oil in a nonstick frying pan. Taking about 1–2 tablespoons at a time, sauté the potato mixture into little potato rösti cakes.

**3** The potato rösti cakes can be served with either apple compote, cranberries or smoked salmon, as desired.

# Baked tomatoes with sheep's milk cheese

Preparation time **approx. 15 minutes** | plus baking time **approx. 20 minutes** | ready in **approx. 35 minutes**
Quick and easy | per portion **approx. 322 kcal/1348 kJ, 19 g P, 24 g F, 6 g CH**

## SERVES 4

750 g tomatoes
1 garlic clove
5 tbsp olive oil
salt
pepper
2 tbsp capers (from a jar)
400 g sheep's milk cheese
1 tbsp fresh thyme leaves

**1** Wash the tomatoes, remove the stalks and slice. Peel and chop the garlic clove. Pre-heat the oven to 200 °C (Gas Mark 6, fan oven 180 °C).

**2** Grease a baking dish with 2 tablespoons of olive oil, then arrange a layer of sliced tomato in the bottom of the dish. Season with salt and pepper, then sprinkle with the drained capers and chopped garlic.

**3** Slice the sheep's milk cheese and spread this over the tomato layer. Drizzle the remaining olive oil over the top and sprinkle with thyme leaves. Bake in the oven for about 20 minutes.

## TIP!!

Goat's milk cheese may be used instead of sheep's milk cheese. You could also replace half the tomatoes with strips of sliced bell pepper.

# Sliced meatloaf with fried egg and fried potatoes

Preparation time **approx. 30 minutes** | plus cooking time **approx. 20 minutes** | ready in **approx. 50 minutes**
Moderate | per portion approx. 781 kcal/3264 kJ, 26 g P, 61 g F, 30 g CH

## SERVES 4

750 g potatoes
salt
pepper
5 tbsp clarified butter
4 slices of meatloaf
2 tbsp butter
4 eggs
2 pickled gherkins

**1** Ideally, wash the potatoes and boil in their skins for about 20 minutes the day before they are needed. Pour off the water, then set aside to drain and cool.

**2** Next day, peel and dice the boiled potatoes. Heat 3 tablespoons of clarified butter in a frying pan, sauté the diced potato on all sides until crisp and season with salt. When cooked, season to taste with pepper.

**3** Meanwhile, heat the remaining clarified butter in another frying pan and sauté the slices of meatloaf on both sides until golden brown. Remove from the pan and keep warm in an oven pre-heated to 60 °C.

**4** Melt the butter in the frying pan and fry the eggs, one at a time. Season with salt and pepper. Top each slice of meatloaf with a fried egg and serve with fried potatoes and sliced gherkins.

## TIP!!

The potatoes may also be cooked the same day but should always be allowed to cool before frying.

# "Strammer max" (ham and fried egg on bread)

Preparation time **approx. 20 minutes**

Quick and easy | per portion **approx. 350 kcal/1470 kJ, 16 g P, 21 g F, 21 g CH**

## SERVES 4

4 slices of farmhouse bread
40 g butter
4 slices of cooked ham
2 tbsp oil
4 eggs
salt
pepper
½ bunch chives
2 pickled gherkins

**1** Butter the slices of bread and top with a slice of cooked ham.

**2** Heat the oil in a frying pan and fry the 4 eggs, one after the other. Season with salt and pepper. Lay a fried egg on top of each slice of ham.

**3** Wash the chives, shake dry and slice into tiny rings. Slice the gherkins or cut into fan shapes. Garnish the ham and fried eggs with chives and gherkins and serve immediately.

## TIP!!

A variation of this dish is to include a slice of cheese between the ham and the fried egg

A hearty treat!

# Sausage meat salad

Preparation time **approx. 20 minutes** | plus marinating time **approx. 20 minutes** | ready in **approx. 40 minutes**
Quick and easy | per portion **approx. 667 kcal/2791 kJ, 19 g P, 64 g F, 4 g CH**

## SERVES 4

750 g cooked sausage meat
2 onions
1 pickled gherkin
1 apple
3 tbsp vinegar
4 tbsp sunflower oil
salt
pepper
½ bunch flat-leaf parsley

**1** Cut the cooked sausage meat into slices, then into strips. Peel the onions, slice into rings and cut the gherkins into thin batons. Peel and quarter the apple, remove the core and finely dice the fruit.

**2** Transfer all the ingredients to a bowl. To make the dressing, combine the vinegar, oil, salt and pepper and drizzle over the salad ingredients. Mix well and leave to marinate for 20 minutes. Wash the parsley, pat dry, tear the leaves off the stems and finely chop. Sprinkle the salad with parsley to serve.

# Fried vegetable patties

Preparation time approx. 30 minutes

Quick and easy | per portion approx. 185 kcal/773 kJ, 11 g P, 12 g F, 5 g CH

## SERVES 4

200 g carrots
400 g courgettes
3 shallots
1 garlic clove
1 tbsp rosemary needles
4 eggs
3 tbsp cream
2 tbsp freshly grated Parmesan
salt
pepper
2 tbsp olive oil

**1** Trim and peel the carrots; trim, wash and dry the courgettes; peel the shallots. Then coarsely grate all the ingredients, transfer them into a bowl and add the peeled and crushed garlic.

**2** Wash, dry and chop the rosemary, then add to the mixture. Blend the eggs, cream and Parmesan together and season with salt and pepper. Add to the vegetable mixture.

**3** Heat the oil in a frying pan. Shape the vegetable mixture into round pancakes and fry in hot oil on both sides until crisp and golden. Remove from the frying pan and drain on kitchen towel. Serve immediately.

# Almost like pizza

# Tuna toast

Preparation time **approx. 25 minutes**

Quick and easy | per portion **approx. 353 kcal/1483 kJ, 14 g P, 27 g F, 14 g CH**

## SERVES 4

4 slices bread, for toasting
2 tbsp butter
1 tin of tuna fish in spring water
  (drained weight 150 g)
3 tomatoes
4 slices of cheese
2 stems parsley, to garnish

**1** Pre-heat the oven to 225 °C (Gas Mark 7, fan oven 200° C). Toast the bread in a toaster, then leave to cool slightly. Butter the toast and place the slices on a baking sheet lined with baking paper.

**2** Drain the tuna in a sieve. Wash 2 tomatoes, remove the stalks and cut into slices. Divide the tuna and tomatoes between the slices of toast and top with a slice of cheese.

**3** Place the baking sheet in the centre of the oven and bake the toasted bread until the cheese has melted.

**4** Wash and dry the remaining tomato and parsley. Garnish each slice of toast with a wedge of tomato and a sprig of parsley.

# Cheese-topped anchovy toast

Preparation time **approx. 15 minutes** | plus baking time **approx. 10 minutes** | ready in **approx. 25 minutes**
Quick and easy | per portion **approx. 190 kcal/798 kJ, 13 g P, 13 g F, 5 g CH**

## SERVES 4

2 tomatoes
1 tbsp capers
4 slices of white bread
2 tbsp butter
8 anchovy fillets, in oil
½ tsp dried oregano
salt
pepper
100 g freshly grated Gruyère
fat, for greasing the baking
   sheet

**1** Pre-heat the oven to 200 °C (Gas Mark 6, fan oven 180 °C). Wash the tomatoes, remove the stalks, then cut into slices. Chop the capers.

**2** Butter the slices of bread. Top each one with tomato slices, 2 anchovy fillets and a few capers. Season with oregano, salt and pepper, and sprinkle with grated cheese.

**3** Arrange the bread on a greased baking sheet and bake in the oven for about 10 minutes. Serve hot.

# Turkey and pesto roll

Preparation time **approx. 15 minutes** | plus cooking time **approx. 15 minutes** | ready in **approx. 30 minutes**
Quick and easy | per portion **approx. 212 kcal/890 kJ, 37 g P, 4 g F, 4 g CH**

## SERVES 4

4 turkey escalopes
150 g pesto (from a jar)
2 tbsp olive oil
125 ml vegetable stock
a few basil leaves

**1** Wash and dry the escalopes, beat until flattened, then spread with a layer of pesto. Roll up the escalopes and secure with a wooden cocktail stick.

**2** Heat the oil in a frying pan and brown the turkey rolls well on all sides. Pour in the stock and simmer the rolls for another 12 minutes until fully cooked.

**3** Divide the turkey rolls into slices, as desired, and serve garnished with fresh basil. Fresh bread and salad make an excellent accompaniment to this dish.

## TIP!!

If you do not have a steak hammer with which to flatten the meat, you can use a heavy frying pan or saucepan instead.

For those with rustic tastes

# Macaroni ham

Preparation time **approx. 30 minutes**
Quick and easy | per portion **approx. 875 kcal/3659 kJ, 35 g P, 40 g F, 95 g CH**

## SERVES 4

500 g macaroni
salt
1 onion
1 garlic clove
150 g cooked ham
150 g smoked bacon
2 tbsp oil
2 eggs
75 g freshly grated Emmental
pepper
paprika powder
2 tbsp freshly chopped parsley

**1** Cook the macaroni in boiling water as indicated on the packet until just firm to the bite. Peel and finely dice the onion and garlic clove. Dice the ham and bacon.

**2** Heat the oil in a frying pan, then gently fry the onion, garlic, ham and bacon. Blend the eggs and cheese together, then season with salt, pepper and paprika powder.

**3** Pour the water off the pasta and allow to drain. Add the pasta and egg and cheese mixture to the ham and bacon in the frying pan and cook until the eggs begin to set. Keep stirring constantly to prevent the ingredients sticking to the bottom of the pan and burning. Serve sprinkled with chopped parsley.

# Spaghetti aglio olio

Preparation time **approx. 15 minutes** | plus cooking time **approx. 10 minutes** | ready in **approx. 25 minutes**
Quick and easy | per portion approx. 493 kcal/2070 kJ, 13 g P, 18 g F, 70 g CH

## SERVES 4

400 g spaghetti
½ fresh chilli pepper
60 ml extra virgin olive oil
4 garlic cloves
1 dried chilli pepper
1 bunch parsley
salt
pepper

**1** Cook the spaghetti until *al dente*, according to the instructions on the packet. Wash, de-seed and chop the chilli pepper. Wash the parsley, shake it dry and chop finely.

**2** Heat the olive oil in a saucepan and gently fry the chopped chilli pepper for 2 minutes. Peel and chop the garlic cloves, then add to the pan and fry for another minute. Do not allow the garlic to brown otherwise it will taste bitter. Crumble the dried chilli pepper ino the pan.

**3** Drain the spaghetti in a sieve. Add the spaghetti and parsley to the garlic and chilli oil mixture in the saucepan and mix the ingredients well. Season to taste with salt and pepper and serve immediately.

## TIP!!

You can always vary the amount of chilli you use, depending on how hot and spicy you like your food.

# Penne all'arrabbiata

Preparation time **approx. 20 minutes** | plus cooking time **approx. 10 minutes** | ready in **approx. 30 minutes**

Quick and easy | per portion **approx. 590 kcal/2470 kJ, 19 g P, 17 g F, 88 g CH**

## SERVES 4

400 g penne
salt
300 g peas, frozen
1 garlic clove
30 g tomato purée
2 tsp capers
2 tbsp olive oil
pepper
pinch of sugar
1 red chilli pepper
½ bunch parsley
80 g black olives, pitted
40 g Parmesan

**1** Cook the penne in boiling, salted water until just firm to the bite. Four minutes before the penne is cooked, add the peas to the pasta.

**2** Meanwhile, peel and chop the garlic clove. Purée the garlic, tomato paste, capers and olive oil together, then season with salt, pepper and sugar.

**3** Clean, wash, de-seed and finely chop the chilli pepper. Stir into the purée. Wash the parsley, then shake dry and chop the leaves. Pour the water off the pasta and peas, then combine immediately with the chilli sauce, black olives and parsley. Top with a sprinkling of grated Parmesan.

## TIP !!

*Arrabbiata* literally means "angry" or "passionate" in Italian – a title which almost certainly refers to the fiery hot chilli pepper it contains.

# Spaghetti with cheese sauce

Preparation time approx. 30 minutes
Quick and easy | per portion approx. 695 kcal/2913 kJ, 30 g P, 30 g F, 77 g CH

## SERVES 4

400 g spaghetti
salt
1 onion
1 tbsp butter or margarine
1 tbsp flour
375 ml milk
50 g Gruyère
50 g Gouda
50 g Parmesan
pepper, freshly ground
nutmeg, freshly grated
50 g pine kernels
1 tbsp thyme leaves

**1** Cook the spaghetti in plenty of boiling, salted water according to the instructions on the packet, then pour off the water and allow to drain thoroughly.

**2** Meanwhile, peel and very finely dice the onion. Heat the butter or margarine in a saucepan and sweat the diced onion until translucent. Dust with flour and continue to fry. Add the milk and mix well. Cook over a low heat for 5 minutes, stirring occasionally.

**3** Finely grate the Gruyère, Gouda and 40 g Parmesan, then add to the sauce and cook over a gentle heat until melted, stirring constantly. Season with salt, pepper and nutmeg.

**4** Lightly toast the pine kernels in a dry frying pan without fat. Mix the spaghetti and cheese sauce together, then serve sprinkled with pine kernels, the rest of the grated Parmesan and thyme leaves.

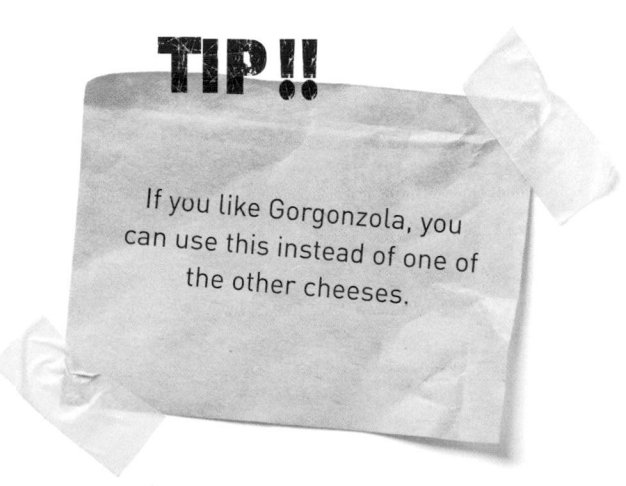

## TIP!!

If you like Gorgonzola, you can use this instead of one of the other cheeses.

# Penne with tomato and tuna sauce

Preparation time **approx. 35 minutes**

Moderate | per portion approx. 739 kcal/3090 kJ, 36 g P, 28 g F, 80 g CH

## SERVES 4

400 g penne
salt
2 onions
1–2 garlic cloves
2–3 dried chilli peppers
3 tbsp oil
1 large tin of peeled tomatoes
   (850 g)
50 g black olives
50 g capers (from a jar)
pepper
1 tbsp sugar
1 bunch flat-leaf parsley
2 tins tuna

**1** Cook the pasta in plenty of boiling, salted water according to the instructions on the packet. Meanwhile peel and finely dice the onions and garlic. Finely chop the chillis. Sauté the onions in hot until until translucent. Add the garlic and chilli and fry over a moderate heat.

**2** Add the tomatoes in their juice and cook uncovered for approx. 10 minutes to reduce the liquid. Pit the olives and add to the sauce along with the drained capers. Season to taste with salt, pepper and sugar.

**3** Wash, dry and finely chop the parsley. Drain the tuna and fork it apart into chunks. Stir the parsley and tuna into the sauce, then serve with the pasta.

## TIP !!

Make absolutely sure you wash your hands after chopping the chilli peppers! Better still, wear kitchen gloves when handling chillis!

# Fried potatoes with bacon

Preparation time **approx. 20 minutes** | plus cooking time **approx. 20 minutes** | plus cooling time **approx. 30 minutes**
ready in **approx. 1 hour 10 minutes**
Moderate | per portion approx. 243 kcal/1020 kJ, 10 g P, 4 g F, 37 g CH

## SERVES 4

1 kg waxy potatoes
salt
100 g bacon
1 onion
3 tbsp clarified butter
pepper
2 tbsp freshly chopped dill

**1** Wash the potatoes and cook in their skins in boiling, salted water for about 20 minutes. Pour off the water and leave to stand for a little while. Then peel the potatoes and allow to cool. Slice the potatoes.

**2** Dice the bacon very finely. Peel and finely chop the onion. Heat the clarified butter in a cast-iron frying pan until very hot, then add the potato slices. Brown the underside, then shake the pan to turn the potatoes over to brown on the other side.

**3** Add the bacon and onion to the potatoes and continue to cook all the ingredients together. Sauté the potatoes until golden brown, season with salt and pepper and serve sprinkled with dill.

crisp
&
hearty

# Stuffed meatballs

Preparation time approx. 30 minutes | plus baking time approx. 20 minutes | ready in approx. 50 minutes
Moderate | per portion approx. 298 kcal/1252 kJ, 22 g P, 23 g F, 2 g CH

## SERVES 4

750 g minced meat, mixed
2 eggs
salt
pepper
½ tsp cayenne pepper
2 tbsp freshly chopped parsley
1 red and 1 green bell pepper
1 tbsp butter
1 tbsp vinegar
1 handful rocket leaves
8 slices processed cheese

**1** Pre-heat the oven to 200 °C (Gas Mark 6, fan oven 180 °C). Mix the minced meat with the eggs, seasonings and parsley. Shape the meat mixture into 8 rounds and arrange these on a baking sheet. Bake in the oven for about 20 minutes.

**2** Wash, trim and de-seed the bell peppers, then dice into small chunks. Fry for about 3 minutes in hot butter. Add the vinegar and 2 tablespoons of water and cook for one more minute. Wash the rocket salad and spin dry.

**3** Slice the meatballs in half. Top the bottom half with rocket leaves and diced bell pepper. Replace the top half and cover with a slice of melting cheese. Cook under a hot grill until the cheese is melted and turns golden brown. Serve with an accompaniment of bread or fried potatoes.

# Beefsteaks with fried onion rings

Preparation time **approx. 20 minutes** | plus frying time **approx. 10 minutes** | ready in **approx. 30 minutes**
Moderate | per portion approx. 593 kcal/2489 kJ, 43 g P, 38 g F, 19 g CH

## SERVES 4

4 tbsp clarified butter
4 beefsteaks (180 g each)
2 onions
100 g flour
500 ml oil, for frying
salt

**1** Heat the clarified butter in a large cast-iron frying pan until very hot. Sear the steaks on both sides for about 2–3 minutes so that the meat is nicely browned on the outside but pink (medium) and juicy on the inside. Remove the cooked steaks from the frying pan and keep warm in an oven heated to approx. 60 °C.

**2** Peel and slice the onions very thinly. Coat the onion rings in flour. Heat the frying oil in a high-sided saucepan or a deep-fat fryer to approx. 180 °C and fry the onion rings for about 10 minutes. Lift out using a slotted spoon and drain on kitchen paper. Season with salt to taste. Serve the steaks with fried onion rings.

# Taco shells with bean and minced meat filling

Preparation time approx. 30 minutes | plus baking time approx. 15 minutes | ready in approx. 45 minutes
Moderate | per portion approx. 886 kcal/3722 kJ, 52 g P, 36 g F, 50 g CH

**SERVES 4**

2 onions
2 garlic cloves
2 yellow bell peppers
1 red chilli pepper
4 tbsp oil
100 ml red salsa
400 g minced beef
500 g kidney beans (tinned)
salt
pepper
½ tsp cumin
8 taco shells (ready-made)
200 g freshly grated Emmental

**1** Peel and chop the onion and garlic. Clean, de-seed, wash and finely chop the chilli. Heat the oil and gently fry the onions and garlic. Add the minced beef, peppers and chilli, then cook all the ingredients for 5 minutes. Drain the liquid off the kidney beans and add to the frying pan. Season the mixture with salt, pepper, and cumin and stir in the salsa. Simmer for another 5 minutes.

**2** Pre-heat the oven to 200 °C (Gas Mark 6, fan oven 180 °C). Fill the taco shells with the meat and bean mixture, then sprinkle with cheese. Bake in the oven for about 15 minutes.

# Schnitzel alla Caprese with mozzarella

Preparation time **approx. 30 minutes**

Moderate | per portion **approx. 690 kcal/2898 kJ, 62 g P, 36 g F, 26 g CH**

## SERVES 4

1 onion
2 garlic cloves
6 tomatoes
3 tbsp olive oil
3 tbsp balsamic vinegar
salt
pepper
4 chicken escalopes
100 g flour
3 eggs
1 tbsp milk
100 g fine breadcrumbs, for
    coating
3 tbsp clarified butter
400 g mozzarella
basil, to garnish

Tomato and mozzarella — something a bit different!

**1** Peel and slice the onions into rings, peel and chop the garlic. Wash the tomatoes, remove the stalks and cut into slices.

**2** Combine the tomato slices with the onion rings and garlic. Prepare a dressing by blending together the oil, balsamic vinegar, garlic, salt and pepper, and drizzle this over the tomato and onion mixture.

**3** Beat the chicken escalopes until flat, then season with salt and pepper. Tip the flour onto a plate. Lightly whisk the eggs and milk together and transfer to a second plate, then tip the breadcrumbs onto a third plate. Taking one escalope at a time, dip each one first in flour, then in the egg mixture and finally in the breadcrumbs.

**4** Heat the oil in a frying pan, then sauté the schnitzel on both sides for about 5 minutes. Slice the mozzarella and arrange on 4 plates along with the tomatoes. Arrange the schnitzels on a bed of tomatoes and cheese. Serve with a garnish of basil leaves.

**Tastes great anywhere, not just in Berlin!**

# Berlin-style calf's liver

Preparation time **approx. 30 minutes**

Moderate | per portion **approx. 305 kcal/1281 kJ, 31 g P, 9 g F, 24 g CH**

## SERVES 4

4 tart apples
2 tbsp butter
2 large onions
4 slices calf's liver
  (each 2–3 cm thick)
1 tbsp flour
1 tbsp oil
salt
pepper

**1** Peel and quarter the apples, cut out the cores, and slice. Fry the sliced apples in a frying pan in 1 tablespoon of butter. Remove from the pan, then keep warm in an oven heated to 60 °C.

**2** Peel and slice the onions, then gently fry in the remaining butter until golden brown. Rinse the liver in running water, pat dry, remove any sinews and tubes and coat in a little flour. Pour the oil into a frying pan and fry the liver on each side for 2–3 minutes. Now (and not before, or the liver will become tough!) season with salt and pepper.

**3** Serve the liver with the apples and onions arranged over the top and drizzle with the cooking juices. Mashed potato makes a perfect accompaniment to this dish.

# Carrot and potato mash

Preparation time **approx. 25 minutes** | plus cooking time **approx. 20 minutes** | ready in **approx. 45 minutes**

**Moderate** | per portion **approx. 250 kcal/1030 kJ, 6 g P, 11 g F, 33 g CH**

## SERVES 4

1 small, red onion
1 kg carrots
30 g butter
½ tsp sugar
salt
pepper
50 ml chicken stock
500 g potatoes
1 bunch flat-leaf parsley
50 ml cream

**1** Peel and finely chop the onion. Clean, peel and roughly dice the carrots. Sweat the onion in the butter in a saucepan until translucent. Add the carrots, cover with a lid and cook for a few minutes. Sprinkle in the sugar and cook, stirring constantly, until the carrots begin to caramelise. Season well with salt and pepper and pour in the chicken stock. Cover the pan with a lid and cook all the ingredients for about 20 minutes until soft, stirring occasionally.

**2** Meanwhile, peel and roughly dice the potatoes. Cook for 20 minutes until tender in plenty of salted water, drain off the water, then add to the carrots. Mash half the carrot and potato mixture and return the mash to the rest of the carrots and potatoes. Wash the parsley, shake dry and chop finely. Add the cream and parsley to the carrots and potatoes, then season to taste.

## TIP !!

This carrot dish will taste even more delicious if served with diced, fried bacon.

# Matjes herring with apples

Preparation time approx. 20 minutes | plus soaking time approx. 2 hours | ready in approx. 2 hours 20 minutes
Quick and easy | per portion approx. 540 kcal/2220 kJ, 23 g P, 44 g F, 14 g CH

## SERVES 4

8 Matjes herring fillets
500 ml milk
2 tart apples
1 tsp lemon juice
4 onions
250 ml cream
150 g yoghurt
pinch of sugar
3 stems dill

**1** Soak the herring fillets for 2 hours in the milk. Peel and core the apples, then slice the fruit and sprinkle with lemon juice. Peel and slice the onions into rings.

**2** Combine the cream, yoghurt and sugar. Add the sliced apple and onion rings. Cut the matjes fillets into wide strips and add to the cream mixture.

**3** Wash the dill, shake dry, tear off the dill tips and add to the herring dish. Serve with dark rye bread.

## TIP !!

In northern Germany, this classic herring dish is traditionally served with potatoes in their skins, green beans and fried bacon bits.

# Breadcrumbed pollock fillets

Preparation time **approx. 25 minutes**

Quick and easy | per portion approx. 435 kcal/1827 kJ, 40 g P, 10 g F, 43 g CH

## SERVES 4

4 pollock fillets
salt
pepper
1 egg
1 tbsp lemon juice
6 tbsp flour
50 g fine breadcrumbs, for
   coating
oil, for frying

**1** Wash the fish fillets, pat dry and rub with salt, pepper and lemon juice. Lightly beat the egg. Tip the egg, flour and breadcrumbs onto separate plates. Coat the fish in turn in the flour, beaten egg and breadcrumbs.

**2** Heat a generous amount of oil in a large frying pan and fry each fillet for about 3 minutes on each side. Remove from the pan and drain on kitchen towel.

Quick
&
simple

# Salmon fillet with herb and mustard topping

Preparation time **approx. 15 minutes** | plus cooking time **approx. 20 minutes** | ready in **approx. 35 minutes**
Quick and easy | per portion approx. 382 kcal/1604 kJ, 38 g P, 24 g F, 2 g CH

## SERVES 4

800 g salmon fillets
1 tbsp lemon juice
salt
pepper
bunch each of dill, chives
    and parsley
150 g crème fraîche
5 tbsp fish stock
2 tsp mustard

**1** Wash the salmon, pat dry and sprinkle with lemon juice. Sprinkle with salt and pepper and place in an ovenproof dish. Pre-heat the oven to 200 °C (Gas Mark 6, fan oven 180 °C).

**2** Wash the herbs, shake dry and chop finely. Combine three-quarters of the herbs with the crème fraîche, stock and mustard and spread this mixture oven the fish. Cook the salmon in the oven for about 20 minutes. Serve sprinkled with the rest of the herbs.

A delicious oven dish

# Pollock and spinach au gratin

Preparation time **approx. 25 minutes** | plus cooking time **approx. 20 minutes** | ready in **approx. 45 minutes**
Moderate | per portion **approx. 530 kcal/2226 kJ, 51 g P, 32 g F, 6 g CH**

## SERVES 4

250 g frozen spinach
1 onion
2 tbsp olive oil
salt
pepper
grated nutmeg
750 g pollock fillets
50 g butter
3 tbsp flour
350 ml fish stock
50 ml cream
100 g Parmesan
fat, for greasing

**1** Defrost the spinach. Peel and chop the onions, then fry gently in hot olive oil. Add the spinach and continue to cook, stirring constantly. Season with salt, pepper and nutmeg.

**2** Pre-heat the oven to 200 °C (Gas Mark 6, fan oven 180 °C). Place the spinach in a greased baking dish and lay the fish on top. Melt the butter in a frying pan and stir in the flour. Add the fish stock and cream, then season with salt and pepper.

**3** Grate the Parmesan. Simmer the sauce until reduced a little, then stir in half the Parmesan. Pour the sauce over the fish, sprinkle the remaining cheese over the top and bake in the oven for about 15 minutes. Finally, place the dish under a hot grill for 5 minutes until the topping is golden brown.

# Mexican-style fish

Preparation time **approx. 10 minutes** | plus baking time **approx. 20 minutes** | ready in **approx. 30 minutes**
Quick and easy | per portion **approx. 445 kcal/1869 kJ, 45 g P, 20 g F, 21 g CH**

## SERVES 4

800 g fish fillet of choice
250 ml salsa, to taste (mild or
   hot)
125 g freshly grated cheddar
50 g corn tortilla chips, plain
1 avocado
100 g sour cream
fat, for greasing

**1** Pre-heat the oven to 200 °C (Gas Mark 6, fan oven 180 °C). Grease a shallow baking dish. Pat the fish dry and place in the dish. Spread with salsa and sprinkle with cheese. Crumble the tortilla chips and sprinkle over the top. Bake the fish in the oven for about 20 minutes.

**2** Meanwhile, peel the avocado, remove the stone and slice the avocado flesh. Serve the baked fish topped with sour cream and sliced avocado. Rice makes a great accompaniment to this fish dish.

## TIP!!

You can tell when an avocado is ripe when the flesh yields to gentle pressure when pressed with the thumb.

# Hearty classics

# Lentil hotpot with smoked pork sausage

Preparation time **approx. 30 minutes** | plus cooking time **approx. 30 minutes** | ready in **approx. 1 hour**
Moderate | per portion approx. 477 kcal/2003 kJ, 34 g P, 15 g F, 49 g CH

## SERVES 4

250 g dried lentils
1.25 l vegetable stock
1 onion
1 bay leaf
2 cloves
bunch of soup vegetables
400 g potatoes
150 g smoked bacon
salt
pepper
white wine vinegar, to taste
4 smoked pork sausages
2 tbsp freshly chopped parsley

**1** Place the lentils in a saucepan with the stock. Peel the onion, stud the onion with cloves and bay leaf, then add to the lentils and bring to a boil. Skim off the froth and cook the lentils for about 15 minutes.

**2** Trim and wash the soup vegetables. Peel and dice the celery and carrots. Slice the leek into rings. Peel and dice the potatoes. Dice the bacon and fry in a frying pan until crisp. Remove the fried bacon from the pan. Fry the vegetables and potatoes in the bacon fat, then add them to the lentils and cook the stew for another 30 minutes. Season to taste with salt, pepper and vinegar. Remove the onion from the pot.

**3** Rinse the sausages, pat dry, add to the pot and heat in the lentil stew for the last 10 minutes of cooking time. Serve garnished with parsley.

## TIP!!

You can obviously use other types of sausage, such as bockwurst, frankfurters or cabanossi.

# Butcher's platter

Preparation time **approx. 25 minutes** | plus cooking time **approx. 1 hour** | ready in **approx. 1 hour 25 minutes**
Moderate | per portion **approx. 1216 kcal/5091 kJ, 30 g P, 121 g F, 2 g CH**

## SERVES 4

1 onion
1 tbsp clarified butter
500 g sauerkraut
250 ml vegetable stock
1 tbsp caraway seeds
1 tsp dill seeds
10 juniper berries
1 bay leaf
4 slices of pork belly
2 liver sausages
2 blood sausages
salt

**1** Peel and finely chop the onions. Heat the clarified butter in a saucepan and sweat the onions until translucent. Add the sauerkraut and cook for a few minutes before pouring in the vegetable stock. Add the spices and seasonings. Lay the pork belly on top of the sauerkraut mixture, cover the pan with a lid and simmer for 45 minutes.

**2** Add the sausages to the saucepan, nestle in amongst the sauerkraut and heat for about 15 minutes. Season the sauerkraut with salt to taste. Arrange the sauerkraut, pork belly and sausages on a large platter and serve with fresh bread or potatoes.

The ultimate in hearty eating!

# Meatloaf

Preparation time approx. 30 minutes | plus cooking time approx. 1 hour | ready in approx. 1 hour 30 minutes
Quick and easy | per portion approx. 482 kcal/2024 kJ, 33 g P, 35 g F, 8 g CH

## SERVES 4

1 bread roll, one day old
2 onions
600 g minced meat, mixed
2 eggs
2 tbsp freshly chopped parsley
2 tsp mustard
salt
pepper
sweet paprika powder
2 tbsp oil

**1** Pre-heat the oven to 200 °C (Gas Mark 6, fan oven 180 °C). Soak the roll in a little water. Peel and chop the onions. Squeeze the water out of the bread roll, then add to the minced meat, onions, eggs and parsley, and knead the ingredients until the mixture is smooth. Season with mustard, salt, pepper and paprika powder, then shape the mixture into a loaf.

**2** Heat the the oil in a frying pan and brown the meatloaf well on all sides. Place in the oven and cook for about 1 hour.

**3** Serve the meatloaf with tomato sauce or gravy made from the meat juices. Fried potatoes make the perfect accompaniment to this dish.

# Schnitzel on toast with mushrooms

Preparation time approx. 30 minutes | plus baking time approx. 10 minutes | ready in approx. 40 minutes
Moderate | per portion approx. 698 kcal/2927 kJ, 53 g P, 25 g F, 65 g CH

## SERVES 4

2 spring onions
150 g button mushrooms
4 pork escalopes
salt
pepper
4 tbsp flour
2 eggs
100 g fine breadcrumbs, for coating
8 slices of wholemeal bread, toasted
3 tbsp clarified butter
4 tbsp cream
150 g freshly grated Emmental
fat, for greasing the baking sheet

**1** Pre-heat the oven to 200 °C (Gas Mark 6, fan oven 180 °C). Trim, wash and dry the spring onions, then slice into rings. Trim and wipe the mushrooms with a damp cloth, then slice.

**2** Wash and dry the pork escalopes, then beat them flat using a steak hammer. Season with salt and pepper and cut in half across the middle. Dip the escalopes one at a time first in flour, then in beaten egg and finally in the breadcrumbs.

**3** Arrange the toasted wholemeal slices on a greased baking sheet. Fry the escalopes in a frying pan in 2 tablespoons of heated clarified butter for about 5 minutes on each side. Remove from the pan, dab off the excess fat and place on the slices of toast.

**4** Heat the rest of the butter along with the juices left in the frying pan and fry the spring onions and mushrooms. Season with salt and pepper and stir in the cream. Divide the mushroom mixture between the slices of toast and sprinkle with Emmental. Bake the toast in the oven for about 10 minutes until the topping is golden brown.

## TIP !!

Mushrooms should never be washed or they will absorb too much water and lose their flavour. Moisten a piece of kitchen towel and carefully wipe off any dirt.

# Spare ribs with honey

Preparation time **approx. 30 minutes** | plus marinating time **approx. 3 hours** | ready in **approx. 3 hours 30 minutes**
Moderate | per portion **approx. 920 kcal/3864 kJ, 45 g P, 57 g F, 54 g CH**

## SERVES 4

1.5 kg spare ribs
2 garlic cloves
5 tbsp olive oil
3 tbsp soy sauce
3 tbsp honey
juice of 1 lemon
2 tbsp brown sugar
salt
½ tsp cayenne pepper

**1** Wash the spare ribs and pat dry. Cut into portions and place in a shallow dish.

**2** Peel and finely chop the garlic. Combine the oil, soy sauce, honey, lemon juice, sugar, salt and cayenne pepper to make a marinade and pour this over the spare ribs. Leave to marinate for at least 3 hours.

**3** Remove the spare ribs from the marinade and leave them to drain. Cook on a hot barbecue for about 20 minutes until both sides are done. Turn frequently, brushing the ribs with marinade. Foil-baked potatoes with sour cream make a great accompaniment to barbecued spare ribs.

It's BBQ time!

## TIP !!

Goulash is a classic casserole dish which develops its distinctive flavour from simmering the dish for a long time over a low heat. The slow cooking method ensures that the meat is beautifully tender.

# Beef goulash

Preparation time **approx. 20 minutes** | plus cooking time **approx. 1 hour** | ready in **approx. 1 hour 20 minutes**
Moderate | per portion **approx. 660 kcal/2720 kJ, 53 g P, 47 g F, 6 g CH**

## SERVES 4

1 kg stewing beef, cubed
100 g bacon
3 small onions
375 ml meat stock
pepper
salt
½ tsp caraway seeds
pinch of paprika powder
250 g sour cream
1 tbsp flour

**1** Wash the meat and pat dry. Finely dice the bacon. Peel and finely dice the onions. Bring the stock to a boil.

**2** Fry the bacon in a hot saucepan until the fat begins to run. Add the onions and meat to the pot and brown quickly, stirring constantly. Add the salt, pepper, caraway seeds and paprika powder. Pour in the stock and bring back to a boil. Cover the pan with a lid and simmer over a low heat for approx. 1 hour.

**3** Blend the cream and flour together, then add to the goulash to thicken the sauce. Goulash is delicious served with various types of pasta, potatoes or dumplings.

# Oven-roasted lamb shank

Preparation time approx. 30 minutes | plus cooking time approx. 1 hour 40 minutes | ready in approx. 2 hours 10 minutes
Moderate | per portion approx. 598 kcal/2509 kJ, 81 g P, 19 g F, 11 g CH

## SERVES 4

4 lamb shanks, on the bone
bunch of soup vegetables
250 g onions
3 garlic cloves
4 tbsp olive oil
350 ml dry red wine
350 ml lamb stock
2 tbsp tomato paste
2 tbsp rosemary needles
10 sage leaves
2 bay leaves
2 allspice corns
1 tbsp cornstarch
salt
pepper

**1** Wash the lamb shanks and pat dry. Rinse the soup vegetables, peel the carrots and celery, then dice all the ingredients. Peel and dice the onions and garlic cloves.

**2** Pre-heat the oven to 200 °C (Gas Mark 6, fan oven 180 °C). Heat the oil in a cooking pot and brown the lamb well on all sides. Add the vegetables, onions and garlic and cook for a few more minutes before adding the wine and lamb stock. Stir in the tomato paste and add the herbs and spices. Cover with a lid and cook the lamb shanks in the oven for about 1 hour 40 minutes.

**3** Remove the lamb shanks from the pot and strain the sauce through a sieve. Return the liquid to the pot, bring back to a boil and thicken with cornstarch. Season with salt and pepper. Serve the lamb shanks with the sauce and a side dish of roast potatoes.

## TIP!!

The reason for straining the sauce through a sieve is to filter out any floating herbs. The sauce will have absorbed their flavour during the long cooking period.

**Beer you can eat!**

# Beef and ale stew

Preparation time **approx. 25 minutes** | plus cooking time **approx. 1 hour 10 minutes** | ready in **approx. 1 hour 35 minutes**
Moderate | per portion **approx. 506 kcal/2120 kJ, 52 g P, 22 g F, 4 g CH**

## SERVES 4

800 g leg of beef
150 g bacon
2 onions
2 tbsp clarified butter
2 tbsp flour
500 ml ale or stout
salt
pepper
1 tsp dried marjoram
1 bay leaf
3 tbsp freshly chopped parsley
sugar
vinegar

**1** Wash the meat, pat dry and cut into bite-sized pieces. Slice the bacon into strips. Peel and chop the onions.

**2** Heat the butter in a casserole dish, then brown the meat well on all sides. Add the bacon and onions and continue to cook for a short while. Sprinkle in the flour and sauté with the other ingredients. Pour in the ale and bring to a boil, then season with salt, pepper and marjoram. Add the bay leaf, then cover and cook on the hob over a low heat for about 1 hour 10 minutes.

**3** Stir in the parsley, then introduce a sweet-and-sour flavour to the dish by seasoning to taste with sugar and vinegar. Potatoes and red cabbage are perfect companions to serve with this dish.

# Pork loin with sauerkraut

Preparation time **approx. 15 minutes** | plus cooking time **approx. 20 minutes** | ready in **approx. 35 minutes**
**Quick and easy** | per portion approx. 325 kcal/1365 kJ, 24 g P, 22 g F, 8 g CH

## SERVES 4

2 onions
1 tbsp oil
500 g sauerkraut
600 g pork loin, boned
   and sliced
1 bay leaf
5 juniper berries
1 l vegetable stock
salt
pepper

**1** Peel and chop the onions. Heat the oil in a saucepan and gently fry the onions. Pull the sauerkraut apart, add to the pan and continue to cook with the onions.

**2** Wash the meat and pat dry. Nestle the slices of meat amongst the sauerkraut along with the bay leaf and juniper berries. Add the stock, then cover the saucepan with a lid and simmer over a low heat for about 20 minutes.

**3** Season to taste with salt and pepper. Serve with fresh buttered bread and mustard.

# Mustard-glazed pork

Preparation time approx. 25 minutes | plus cooking time approx. 2 hours 30 minutes | ready in approx. 3 hours
Moderate | per portion approx. 510 kcal/2142 kJ, 57 g P, 28 g F, 6 g CH

## SERVES 4

1 kg neck of pork
1 tbsp mustard
salt
pepper
¼ tsp paprika powder
100 g smoked bacon
2 onions
125 ml meat stock
2 tbsp sour cream
2 tbsp crème fraîche
2 tbsp flour

**1** Wash the meat, pat dry and spread with mustard. Sprinkle with salt, pepper and paprika powder. Dice the bacon and fry in a hot, flameproof casserole dish or saucepan until the fat begins to run. Peel and chop the onions, then add them to bacon along with the pork. Brown well in the bacon fat.

**2** Cover with a lid and cook the pork for about 2 ½ hours over a moderate heat. Meanwhile, add the meat stock a little at a time. At the end of the cooking time, remove the meat from the pot and keep warm. Blend the sour cream, crème fraîche and flour together and mix until smooth, then add it to the liquid to thicken the sauce.

**3** Slice the neck of pork and serve with the sauce. Mashed potatoes and Bavarian sauerkraut or red cabbage go well with this dish.

## TIP!!

Mashed potato is very easy to make yourself: boil 1 kg of potatoes, peel off the skins and mash with a potato masher. Stir in 150 ml of milk and grated nutmeg, season with salt and pepper – and it's ready to eat!

# Crispy fried chicken

Preparation time **approx. 25 minutes** | plus frying time **approx. 15 minutes** | ready in **approx. 40 minutes**
Moderate | per portion approx. 1611 kcal/6749 kJ, 148 g P, 95 g F, 18 g CH

## SERVES 4

2 chickens (1.4 kg each)
salt
3 tbsp lemon juice
100 g flour
3 eggs
125 g breadcrumbs
1.5 l oil, for frying
2 unwaxed lemons

**1** Wash the chickens and pat dry. Separate the breasts and cut off the legs. Remove the skin and make a few cuts on the inside of the legs.

**2** Season the chicken pieces with salt and sprinkle with lemon juice. Place the flour, eggs and breadcrumbs on separate plates. Beat the eggs with a little water. Heat the oil in a large saucepan or deep-fat fryer.

**3** Begin by coating the chicken pieces in flour, then dip them in the eggs and finally in the breadcrumbs. Gently press the breadcrumb coating onto the chicken. Fry the chicken in hot oil for about 15 minutes, then drain on kitchen towel. Serve each piece of fried chicken with half a lemon. French fries or potato salad make a delicious accompaniment to fried chicken.

A classic Viennese dish

# Green Cabbage and sausages

Preparation time **approx. 25 minutes** | plus cooking time **approx. 1 hour 10 minutes** | ready in **approx. 1 hour 35 minutes**
Moderate | per portion **approx. 717 kcal/3011 kJ, 50 g P, 48 g F, 20 g CH**

## SERVES 4

1 kg green cabbage
salt
2 onions
2 tbsp goose fat
250 ml vegetable stock
pepper
250 g smoked meat
300 g smoked pork sausages
400 g blood sausage
3 tbsp oat flakes

**1** Clean the cabbage, pull the leaves off the stem, wash and cut away any hard bits. Blanch the cabbage for about 3 minutes in boiling, salted water, then remove and drain before chopping.

**2** Peel and chop the onions. Heat the butter in a saucepan and fry the onions until translucent. Add the cabbage and continue cooking, stirring frequently. Pour in the stock, season the cabbage with salt and pepper and simmer for about 25 minutes.

**3** Once the cabbage is cooked, add the smoked meat, cover with a lid and simmer for another 15 minutes. Add the smoked pork sausage and blood sausage to the cabbage and continue cooking all the ingredients another 20 minutes over a low heat. Stir in the oat flakes and leave them to soak up the liquid for 10 minutes. Season the green cabbage with salt and pepper and serve with boiled potatoes.

## TIP !!

In autumn and winter when green cabbage is in season, it can often be bought already cleaned and pre-packed.

# Minced meat patties

Preparation time **approx. 30 minutes** | plus cooking time **approx. 10 minutes** | ready in **approx. 40 minutes**
Moderate | per portion approx. 492 kcal/2055 kJ, 31 g P, 31 g F, 23 g CH

## SERVES 4

2 bread rolls, one day old
1 onion
½ tbsp butter
500 g minced meat, mixed
½ bunch freshly chopped
   parsley
2 eggs
salt
pepper
½ tsp marjoram
½ tsp sweet paprika powder
2 tbsp clarified butter

**1** Soak the bread rolls in 100 ml of hot water. Peel and finely chop the onions. Heat the butter in a frying pan and gently fry the onions.

**2** Place the minced meat, onions and parsley in a bowl. Squeeze as much water as possible out of the bread rolls and add to the meat mixture. Add the eggs and seasonings and knead all the ingredients by hand into a smooth meat paste.

**3** Moisten your hands, then shape the meat mixture into rounds. Heat the clarified butter in a frying pan and brown quickly on all sides. Reduce the heat and cook for about 10 minutes over a low temperature. Potato salad or sauerkraut salad go well with this dish.

## TIP!!

If preparing a large quantity of meat patties, e.g. for a party, simply place the uncooked patties on a greased baking sheet and bake in the oven for approx. 25 minutes at 180 °C (Gas Mark 4).

# Cevapcici with tzaziki

Preparation time approx. 35 minutes | plus standing time approx. 30 minutes | ready in approx. 1 hour 5 minutes
Moderate | per portion approx. 432 kcal/1814 kJ, 40 g P, 26 g F, 8 g CH

## SERVES 4

½ cucumber
salt
4 garlic cloves
250 g quark (20 % fat)
150 g yoghurt
1 tbsp finely chopped parsley
¼ tsp pepper
1 onion
1 red and 1 green bell pepper
600 g minced beef
1 tsp paprika powder
3 tbsp olive oil

**1** Wash, peel and finely grate the cucumber. Sprinkle with salt and set aside for 15 minutes, then gently press the water out of the grated cucumber.

**2** Meanwhile, peel and finely chop the garlic cloves. Place the quark, yoghurt and one finely chopped garlic clove and grated cucumber in a bowl and mix well. Season to taste with parsley, salt and pepper.

**3** To make the cevapcici, peel and very finely chop the onion. Wash the bell peppers, pat dry, trim, de-seed and cut into strips.

**4** Place the minced beef in a bowl, add the rest of the garlic, salt, pepper and paprika powder, and knead into a dough. Moisten your hands and shape the meat mixture into finger-length sausages, approx. 2 cm thick. Place the cevapcici side by side on a plate, cover and stand in the refrigerator for 30 minutes.

**5** Heat the oil in a nonstick frying pan. Brown the cevapcici on all sides for about 5 minutes, turning frequently. Sprinkled the diced onion over the cevapcici, garnish with pepper strips and dust lightly with a sprinkling of paprika powder. Serve with the tzaziki.

Balkans meet Greece

# Chilli Con Carne

Preparation time **approx. 30 minutes** | plus cooking time **approx. 20 minutes** | ready in **approx. 50 minutes**
Moderate | per portion approx. 450 kcal/ 1880 kJ, 35 g P, 24 g F, 24 g CH

## SERVES 4

500 g red kidney beans (tinned)
850 g tomatoes (tinned)
1 large onion
2 garli cloves
1–2 red chilli peppers
1 red and 1 green bell pepper
2 tbsp olive oil
500 g minced beef
1 tbsp tomato paste
350 ml vegetable stock
salt
pepper
1 tsp sweet paprika powder
½ tsp ground cumin

**1** Tip the kidney beans into a sieve and leave to drain. Dice the tinned tomatoes.

**2** Peel and finely chop the onion and garlic. Wash the chilli peppers, pat dry, cut in half lengthways and remove the seeds, pith and stalks. Slice the peppers diagonally into rings. Wash the bell peppers, cut them in half and remove the stalks, pith and seeds, then dice the flesh.

**3** Heat the olive oil in a saucepan and fry the minced meat until it is grey and crumbly. Push the meat to one side of the pan, then fry the onion, garlic and chilli on the other side.

**4** Stir in the chopped tomatoes, diced bell peppers, beans and tomato paste. Add the stock and chilli, then cover and simmer for approx. 20 minutes over a low heat. Season the chilli with salt, pepper, paprika powder and cumin, and serve with freshly baked baguette or rice.

## TIP!!

When making chilli, it is always a good idea to make twice as much as you need as it tastes even better the next day and also freezes well.

# Hamburgers

Preparation time **approx. 20 minutes** | plus frying time **approx. 10 minutes** | ready in **approx. 30 minutes**
Moderate | per portion **approx. 533 kcal/2237 kJ, 37 g P, 28 g F, 34 g CH**

## SERVES 4

600 g minced beef
50 g oat flakes
2 tbsp ketchup
2 tbsp milk
1 tbsp Dijon mustard
1 egg
salt
pepper
½ tsp dried oregano
2 tbsp oil
1 onion
4 hamburger buns
2 tbsp butter
ketchup, to serve

**1** Mix the minced beef, oat flakes, ketchup, milk, mustard and egg into a meaty dough and knead well. Season well with salt, pepper and oregano.

**2** Shape the mixture into 4 equal rounds. Heat the oil in a frying pan and brown the burgers well on both sides, then cook for about another 7 minutes over a reduced heat.

**3** Peel and slice the onion into rings. Just before the burgers are ready, place onion rings on each burger and cook for a few minutes. Cut the buns in half and spread with butter, then toast under the grill.

**4** Sandwich a burger inside each bun, top the burger with onion rings and serve with ketchup. Garnish to taste with sliced tomato and lettuce.

## TIP!!

Crispy fried bacon makes a delicious burger topping. Add a slice of cheese to turn it into a cheeseburger.

# Pizza Vesuvio

Preparation time approx. 30 minutes | plus proving and baking time approx. 1 hour 20 minutes

ready in approx. 1 hour 50 minutes

Time-consuming | per pizza approx. 453 kcal/1897 kJ, 14 g P, 15 g F, 64 g CH

## MAKES 1 CIRCULAR PIZZA TRAY

250 g flour
1 tsp dry yeast
salt
pepper
5 tbsp olive oil
2 onions
2 garlic cloves
400 g chopped tomatoes
   (tinned)
½ tsp sugar
½ tsp dried oregano
50 g grated pecorino
1 red bell pepper
50 g Gorgonzola
½ red chilli pepper
2 tbsp herb-flavoured oil
fat, for greasing the pizza pan

**1** Make the pizza dough by kneading together the flour, yeast, 100 ml lukewarm water, a pinch of salt and 4 tablespoons of olive oil. Place the dough in a bowl, cover with a cloth and stand in a warm place to prove for about 1 hour.

**2** Peel and chop the onions and garlic, then fry in 1 tablespoon of hot olive oil until translucent. Add the tomatoes; season with salt, pepper, sugar and oregano; then continue to cook until the mixture is reduced to a smooth tomato sauce.  Meanwhile, trim and wash the red pepper, remove the pith and cut into strips.

**3** Pre-heat the oven to 220 °C (Gas Mark7, fan oven 200 °C). Roll out the dough into a round large enough to cover the base of an oiled pizza pan, gently pressing around the outer rim to make a raised edge. Spread the tomato sauce over the pizza base. Top with half the grated pecorino and strips of red pepper. Slice the Gorgonzola into small pieces, finely chop the chilli pepper, then add these to the pizza topping. Sprinkle with the rest of the pecorino and drizzle with herb oil. Bake in the oven for about 20 minutes.

## TIP!!

The pizza topping can obviously be varied to taste!

# Rhineland-style beans and sausage

Preparation time **approx. 30 minutes** | plus cooking time **approx. 25 minutes** | ready in **approx. 55 minutes**
Moderate | per portion approx. 1090 kcal/4490 kJ, 17 g P, 104 g F, 25 g CH

## SERVES 4

500 g green beans
600 g floury potatoes
200 g fatty bacon
1 onion
200 g streaky bacon
1 tbsp butter
½ tsp dried savory
pinch of sugar
4 smoked pork sausages
salt
pepper

**1** Tip the beans into a sieve and rinse in cold water. Leave to drain. Wash, peel and quarter the potatoes, then place in a saucepan with a little salted water. Boil for about 20 to 25 minutes until cooked.

**2** Meanwhile, dice the fatty bacon. Peel and finely chop the onion. Cut the streaky bacon into slices.

**3** Fry the fatty bacon in a large saucepan over a low heat until the fat begins to run. Remove the pieces of bacon from the pan and set aside. Add the butter to the bacon fat in the saucepan, then fry the onion and streaky bacon. Add the beans and just enough hot water to cover the beans. Add the savory and a pinch of sugar.

**4** Cover the beans and simmer over a low heat for approx. 25 minutes. About 10–15 minutes before the end of the cooking time, place the sausages on the beans, then cover and leave to cook for the remainder of the cooking time.

**5** Roughly mash the potatoes using a potato masher. Remove the sausages from the saucepan and blend the mashed potatoes with the beans. Season with salt and pepper and serve with the sausages.

## TIP !!

You can use any variety of green beans for this dish

# Beef roulades in red wine sauce

Preparation time approx. 45 minutes | plus cooking time approx. 1 hour 15 minutes | ready in approx. 2 hours
Time-consuming | per portion approx. 295 kcal/1239 kJ, 40 g P, 10 g F, 6 g CH

## SERVES 4

2 shallots
4 pickled gherkins
4 beef roulades
salt
pepper
4 tsp hot mustard
4 slices of bacon
1 tsp dried thyme
bunch of soup greens
50 g smoked bacon
2 tbsp clarified butter
2 bay leaves
400 ml dry red wine
400 ml meat stock
3 tbsp flour
sour cream, to taste

**1** Peel and slice the shallots into thin rings. Slice the gherkins into thin strips. Wash the meat, pat dry and lay the roulades flat on a clean work surface.

**2** Season the roulades with salt and pepper and spread each one with a teaspoon of mustard. Top each one with a slice of bacon, sprinkle with thyme and top with shallot rings and strips of gherkin. Roll up the roulades and secure with cocktail sticks.

**3** Clean and wash the soup greens, peel the celery and carrots and dice all the ingredients into small pieces. Finely dice the bacon. Heat the butter in a flameproof casserole dish and brown the roulades well. Remove the meat from the dish, add the vegetables and bacon and fry for a few minutes. Return the roulades to the casserole dish along with the bay leaves. Add the wine and stock, cover and cook for approx. 1 hour 15 minutes over a low heat.

**4** Lift the roulades out of the pot and keep warm in an oven heated to 60 °C. Strain the cooking liquid through a sieve, return to the pot and bring to a boil. Mix the flour with 150 ml water and blend well until smooth, then use this to thicken the sauce. Season with salt and pepper. Enrich the sauce with sour cream, to taste. Serve the roulades in the sauce. This dish is delicious served with dumplings, potatoes or pasta.

Just like mum's home cooking!

# Minced-meat-stuffed peppers

Preparation **approx. 30 minutes** | plus cooking time **approx. 30 minutes** | ready in **approx. 1 hour**
Moderate | per portion approx. 530 kcal/2226 kJ, 32 g P, 21 g F, 53 g CH

## SERVES 4

4 large yellow bell peppers
2 onions
2 garlic cloves
2 tbsp butter
1 tbsp dried marjoram
150 g streaky bacon
300 g minced meat, mixed
1 egg
50 g fine breadcrumbs
salt
pepper
1 tsp hot mustard
200 ml vegetable stock
2 tbsp flour
125 ml tomato purée (tinned)
1 tbsp freshly chopped basil

**1** Slice the top off each bell pepper to make a lid. Scoop out the seeds and rinse. Peel and chop the onions and garlic. Heat the butter in a frying pan and gently fry 1 onion and 1 garlic clove. Add the marjoram and fry briefly.

**2** Dice the bacon. Tip the ingredients from the frying pan into a bowl and add the bacon. Add the minced meat, the remaining onion and garlic, egg, breadcrumbs, salt, pepper and mustard, and knead the ingredients into a homogeneous mixture. Pre-heat the oven to 180 °C (Gas Mark 4, fan oven 160 °C).

**3** Spoon the mince mixture into the peppers and replace the lids. Place the peppers in a baking dish, pour in the stock and cook in the oven for about 30 minutes.

**4** Remove the peppers from the baking dish and keep warm. Blend the flour with the cooking liquid, stirring well, to thicken the sauce. Stir in the tomato purée, bring to a boil, then season with salt and pepper. Add the basil and serve the sauce with the stuffed peppers. This dish goes well with rice or rice noodles.

**TIP !!**

You can replace some of the minced meat with cooked rice, if desired.

# Bean and pork stew

Preparation time **approx. 20 minutes** | plus cooking time **approx. 30 minutes** | ready in **approx. 50 minutes**
Moderate | per portion **approx. 322 kcal/1352 kJ, 26 g P, 11 g F, 30 g CH**

## SERVES 4

750 g green beans
600 g small potatoes
300 g pork fillet
1 onion
3 tbsp oil
150 ml meat stock
½ bunch savory
salt

**1** Trim and wash the beans, then cut into small pieces. Peel and wash the potatoes, then cut in half lengthways. Slice the pork fillet into bite-sized pieces. Peel and finely dice the onions.

**2** Heat the oil in a large saucepan and fry the pork. Remove the meat from the pan. Fry the potatoes and onions in the fat left in the saucepan until lightly browned.

**3** Add the beans, meat and stock; bring to a boil; then cook for approx. 30 minutes. Wash the savory, pat dry, finely chop, then add to the pot just before the end of the cooking time. Season the bean stew with salt and serve immediately.

## TIP!!

Using frozen green beans can save time without compromising greatly on flavour. If you choose this option, just add the beans approx. 15 minutes before the end of the cooking time and turn up the heat briefly.

# For special occasions

# Beef Carpaccio with radish sprouts

Preparation time **approx. 20 minutes** | plus freezing time **approx. 1 hour** | ready in **approx. 1 hour 20 minutes**
Quick and easy | per portion **approx. 622 kcal/2612 kJ, 48 g P, 47 g F, 1 g CH**

## SERVES 4

400 g beef (sirloin)
400 g Tyrolean alpine cheese
100 g radish sprouts
150 g rucola
3 tbsp olive oil
2 tbsp balsamic vinegar
salt
pepper
1 tbsp freshly chopped flat-leaf
  parsley

**1** Slice the beef very thinly. To make this easier, chill the meat in the freezer for an hour beforehand. Finely dice the cheese. Wash the radish sprouts and rucola and shake dry.

**2** Arrange the beef slices on a platter, garnish with radish sprouts and rucola, then sprinkle with the diced cheese.

**3** Blend the olive oil and vinegar together, season with salt and pepper and stir in the parsley. Drizzle the dressing over the carpaccio and serve with fresh farmhouse bread.

Simply elegant

**TIP!!**

This recipe for schnitzel can also be made with pork – in which case it would have to be called "Wiener-style schnitzel" instead of "Wiener schnitzel".

# Wiener schnitzel

Preparation time **approx. 30 minutes**

Moderate | per portion **approx. 400 kcal/1670 kJ, 37 g P, 15 g F, 27 g CH**

## SERVES 4

4 veal escalopes (150 g each)
4 tbsp flour
100 g fine breadcrumbs, for coating
2 eggs
salt
pepper
20 g butter
100 ml rapeseed oil
1 unwaxed lemon

**1** Rinse the veal escalopes in cold, running water, then pat dry. Wrap the escalopes in cling film and beat the meat until thin and flat using a steak hammer or a saucepan.

**2** Tip the flour and breadcrumbs onto separate, shallow plates. Beat the eggs in a dish. Season the escalopes on both sides with salt and pepper, then dip first in the flour, then in the beaten egg and finally in the breadcrumbs.

**3** Heat the butter and oil together in a large frying pan and sauté the veal for 2–3 minutes on each side until golden brown. Keep spooning some of the fat in the frying pan over the schnitzels so that they develop a lovely, bubbly crust. As each schnitzel is cooked, keep it warm in an oven heated to 50 °C.

**4** Wash the lemon and wipe dry with a tea towel. Cut into four or eight wedges. Serve the schnitzels garnished with lemon wedges. Fried potatoes, French fries or a warm potato salad all make delicious accompaniments to this dish.

# Spaghetti bolognese

Preparation time **approx. 30 minutes** | plus frying and cooking time **approx. 30 minutes** | ready in **approx. 1 hour**
Moderate | per portion approx. 733 kcal/3079 kJ, 41 g P, 28 g F, 76 g CH

## SERVES 4

1 onion
1 garlic clove
75 g streaky bacon
1 carrot
½ stick celery
2 tbsp olive oil
400 g minced meat, mixed
100 ml stock
salt
pepper
100 ml milk
1 tsp freshly chopped oregano
1 tbsp sugar
400 g chopped tomatoes
  (tinned)
400 g spaghetti
50 g Parmesan, freshly grated
thyme, to garnish

**1** Peel and chop the onion and garlic. Dice the bacon. Peel the carrot, trim and wash the celery, then dice both vegetables. Fry the bacon in hot oil until the fat begins to run. Begin by browning the vegetables well, then add the minced meat, stirring all the time.

**2** Add the stock and bring the mixture a boil. Simmer and reduce the mixture until the liquid has all but disappeared. Season with salt and pepper. Stir in the milk and cook until the ingredients thicken into a smooth, creamy sauce. Blend in the oregano, sugar and tomatoes and gently cook the sauce for 30 minutes over a low temperature.

**3** Cook the spaghetti *al dente* according to the instructions on the packet. Pour off the water and leave to drain properly. Transfer to plates, top each portion with sauce, sprinkle with Parmesan and serve garnished with thyme.

## TIP!!

The sauce can be made even more delicious by adding a glass of red wine to the juices in the pan after the ingredients have been fried. The sauce should also be simmered for longer, ideally for 1 hour.

# Risotto with porcini mushrooms

Preparation time **approx. 40 minutes**

Moderate | per portion **approx. 498 kcal/2092 kJ, 14 g P, 12 g F, 80 g CH**

## SERVES 4

250 g fresh porcini mushrooms
  (or 50 g dried)
1 onion
3 tbsp butter
400 g risotto rice
50 ml white wine
1 l hot vegetable stock
salt
pepper
50 g Parmesan
2 tbsp freshly chopped parsley

**1** Clean the fresh porcini and dice into small pieces (soak dried porcini in 200 ml water). Peel and chop the onion. Heat 2 tablespoons of butter in a frying pan and fry the onion and mushrooms until softened. Add the risotto rice and continue to sauté, stirring constantly, until the rice turns translucent.

**2** Add the white wine to the frying pan. Wait for it to reduce, then add a ladle of the vegetable stock (alternatively you can use a combination of 750 ml stock plus the water used for soaking the porcini). Keep stirring until the rice has almost absorbed all the liquid, then add another 1–2 ladles of stock. Continue in this way until the stock is used up and the rice is creamy. Season with salt and pepper.

**3** Grate the Parmesan, then stir this into the risotto along with the remaining butter and parsley. Serve immediately.

## TIP!!

It is important to use special risotto rice for this recipe as other kinds of rice will not produce such a lovely, creamy texture.

# Venison steak with figs

Preparation time **approx. 30 minutes**

Moderate | per portion **approx. 320 kcal/1344 kJ, 23 g P, 17 g F, 8 g CH**

## SERVES 4

4 venison steaks (100 g each)
2 tbsp clarified butter
salt
pepper
200 ml white wine
3 tbsp fig conserve
150 ml cream
2 figs

**1** Wash the venison steaks and pat dry. Brown on both sides for about 3 minutes in the hot butter. Season with salt and pepper, then keep warm in an oven heated to 50 °C.

**2** Add the white wine to the cooking juices and stir in the fig conserve. Simmer until the the sauce is reduced a little before adding the cream. Season the sauce to taste with salt and pepper.

**3** Wash and slice the figs. Top each steak with half a fig, cut into slices, and serve with the sauce. A side dish of fried potatoes goes extremely well with venison steaks.

# Lamb loin topped with wild garlic

Preparation time approx. 30 minutes

Moderate | per portion approx. 355 kcal/1489 kJ, 18 g P, 21 g F, 24 g CH

## SERVES 4

200 g fresh wild garlic leaves
200 g pine kernels
200 ml olive oil
salt
pepper
1 egg white
50 g fine breadcrumbs
600 g lamb loin fillet

**1** Wash the wild garlic leaves and pat dry. Place in a food processor with the pine kernels, 180 ml olive oil, salt and pepper, and purée. Add the egg white and give all the ingredients another thorough mixing. Add the breadcrumbs to thicken the mixture.

**2** Wash the lamb loin and pat dry. Season with salt and pepper. Heat the remaining oil in a frying pan and brown the lamb for about 3 minutes on each side.

**3** Pre-heat the oven to 220 °C (Gas Mark 7, fan oven 200 °C). Spread a layer of wild garlic paste about 1 cm thick over the lamb. Place in the oven and cook under top heat until golden brown. Cut into slices and serve with green beans.

spicy sophistication

# Beef fillet with beans in sherry sauce

Preparation time **approx. 30 minutes** | plus cooking time **approx. 35 minutes** | ready in **approx. 1 hour**
Moderate | per portion **approx. 582 kcal/2444 kJ, 58 g P, 32 g F, 8 g CH**

## SERVES 4

1 kg fillet of beef
salt
pepper
1 tsp cumin
2 tbsp olive oil
1 garlic clove
50 g Gruyère
20 g almonds, chopped
1 tbsp mustard
750 g green beans
½ bunch savory
2 shallots
100 ml sherry
pinch cayenne pepper

**1** Wash the fillet of beef, pat dry, then rub with salt, pepper and cumin. Heat the olive oil in a flameproof cooking pot and brown the fillet well on all sides.

**2** Pre-heat the oven to 200 °C (Gas Mark 6, fan oven 180 °C). Peel and crush the garlic clove. Grate the Gruyère, then mix the garlic and cheese with the almonds and mustard into a paste. Spread this over the top of the fillet.

**3** Top and tail the beans, wash, then blanch in boiling salted water for approx. 3 minutes. Pour off the water, then allow to drain. Wash the savory, then shake dry. Peel and quarter the shallots. Add all these ingredients to the beef and pour in the sherry. Cover and cook in the oven for about 20 minutes. Remove the lid and cook for another 15 minutes.

**4** Remove the savory, then season the sauce with salt and a little cayenne pepper. Serve the fillet of beef with the green beans and sauce.

Looks very impressive!

# Chicken legs with olives

Preparation time **approx. 25 minutes** | plus cooking time **approx. 45 minutes** | ready in **approx. 1 hour 10 minutes**
Moderate | per portion approx. 462 kcal/1940 kJ, 31 g P, 29 g F, 11 g CH

## SERVES 4

4 chicken legs
80 g black olives, pitted
salt
pepper
4 tbsp olive oil
1 kg tomatoes
2 onions
½ bunch basil
2 garlic cloves
150 ml red wine
3 tbsp tomato paste
1 tbsp honey

**1** Wash the chicken legs, pat dry, then loosen the skin slightly. Slice 40 g olives, slide these under the skin and season the chicken with salt and pepper.

**2** Heat 2 tablespoons of olive oil in a flameproof casserole dish and brown the chicken well. Remove the chicken from the pot. Pre-heat the oven to 200 °C (Gas Mark 6, fan oven 180 °C). Wash and dry the tomatoes, remove the stalks and cut into slices. Peel the onions and slice into rings.

**3** Place the onions and tomatoes in the casserole dish, then season with salt and pepper. Wash the basil, shake dry and cut the leaves into strips. Sprinkle these over the onion and tomato mixture, then drizzle the remaining olive oil over the top. Arrange the chicken legs on this bed of onions and tomatoes and sprinkle the remaining olives over the top.

**4** Place the chicken in the oven and cook for about 45 minutes. Peel and crush the garlic cloves. Mix with the red wine, tomato paste and honey. After the chicken has cooked for 25 minutes, pour this mixture over the chicken. Serve with fresh white bread.

## TIP!!

Always make sure that chicken is properly cooked through. If in doubt, leave in the oven a bit longer. Raw poultry can contain salmonella bacteria, which cause food poisoning.

# Thai wok

Preparation time **approx. 40 minutes**
Moderate | per portion **approx. 380 kcal/1590 kJ, 31 g P, 5 g F, 53 g CH**

## SERVES 4

200 g basmati rice
salt
piece of ginger root (2 cm long)
2 garlic cloves
400 g chicken breast fillets
3 tbsp lemon juice
3 tbsp soy sauce
200 g sugar snap peas
2 red bell peppers
6 sprigs coriander
1 tbsp rapeseed oil
black pepper

**1** Boil the rice in 400 ml water (use a 2:1 ratio of water to rice), salt and cook until firm to the bite for about 15 minutes according to the instructions on the packet. The water should have been completely absorbed by the rice during cooking.

**2** Meanwhile, peel and finely chop the ginger and garlic. Rinse the chicken breasts in cold water and pat dry. Slice the meat into thin strips, then mix with the ginger, garlic, lemon juice and soy sauce.

**3** Wash the sugar snap peas and pat dry. Top and tail the peas, then slice the peas in halves or thirds. Bring a small amount of salted water to a boil and cook the peas for 3 minutes, transfer to a sieve, then shock in cold water.

**4** Wash the bell peppers; cut in half; remove the stalks; pith and seeds; then cut into bite-sized pieces. Wash the coriander and pat dry using kitchen towel. Tear the leaves off the stems and finely chop.

**5** Heat the oil in a wok or a large, nonstick frying pan. Add the chicken and marinade mixture to the wok and fry on all sides until golden brown, stirring all the time. Add the sugar snap peas and peppers and fry for another 3 minutes. Finally stir in the rice and season all the ingredients to taste with salt, pepper and coriander.

# Corn-fed chicken with tarragon and mustard sauce

Preparation time **approx. 35 minutes**

Moderate | per portion **approx. 420 kcal/1764 kJ, 39 g P, 24 g F, 8 g CH**

## SERVES 4

350 g broccoli
350 g Romanesco broccoli
salt
3 shallots
2 stems tarragon
2 corn-fed chicken breasts with
  skin (approx. 400 g each)
2 tbsp oil
2 tbsp butter
1 tbsp flour
400 ml chicken stock
3 tsp Dijon mustard
2 tbsp crème fraîche
pepper
3 tbsp slivered almonds
orange zest spirals, for the
  garnish

**1** Clean and wash the broccoli and Romanesco, divide into small florets. Cover and cook in boiling, salted water for 8–10 minutes. Peel and finely dice the shallots. Wash the tarragon and shake dry before pulling off the leaves. Set aside a few for the garnish, then finely chop the rest.

**2** Cut the chicken breasts, with skin attached, from the bone. Wash and pat dry. Heat the oil in a frying pan. Fry the chicken breasts for 6–8 minutes on all sides, season with salt, remove from the pan and keep warm in an oven heated to 60 °C.

**3** Heat 1 tablespoon of butter in the frying fat. Sweat the shallots, dust with flour and fry gently until golden brown. Add the stock, stirring constantly. Bring the sauce to a boil and simmer for approx. 5 minutes. Stir the tarragon, mustard and crème fraîche into the sauce. Season with salt and pepper.

**4** Toast the almonds until golden in a dry frying pan. Add 1 tablespoon of butter and melt. Drain the broccoli and Romanesco, then coat in the melted butter. Serve on plates, garnishing with orange peel and the rest of the tarragon. Serve with baguette or rice.

**TIP !!**

Corn-fed chickens are chickens which are only fed corn. This gives the meat a yellowish tinge and a better flavour.

# Coq au vin

Preparation time **approx. 30 minutes** | plus marinating time **approx. 12 hours** | plus cooking time **approx. 30 minutes**
ready in **approx. 13 hours**
Time-consuming | per portion **approx. 610 kcal/2562 kJ, 62 g P, 33 g F, 11 g CH**

## SERVES 4

1 chicken, ready to cook
  (approx. 1.2 kg)
3 shallots
3 carrots
50 g celeriac
1 small leek
1 bay leaf
10 peppercorns
1 sprig thyme
1 garlic clove
500 ml red wine
3 tbsp olive oil
1 tbsp tomato paste
2 tbsp cornstarch
salt
pepper

**1** Wash the chicken and pat dry, then divide into 4–8 pieces. Peel and dice the shallots, carrots and celery. Trim and wash the leek, then slice into rings.

**2** Place the chicken pieces in a bowl with the vegetables, bay leaf, peppercorns, thyme and garlic clove. Add enough red wine to cover the ingredients and leave to marinate overnight in the refrigerator.

**3** The following day, remove the chicken pieces from the marinade and pat dry using kitchen towel. Pre-heat the oven to 200 °C (Gas Mark 6, fan oven 180 °C).

**4** Heat the oil in a casserole pot and brown the chicken well. Add the vegetables from the marinade and the tomato paste, cook briefly, then pour in some of the marinade liquid. Continue to cook until the liquid has all but disappeared, then sprinkle in the cornstarch and pour in the rest of the marinade. Cover and cook in the oven for about 30 minutes.

**5** Remove the chicken pieces from the pot, then heat the sauce on the hob to reduce it a little. Remove the bay leaf, thyme and garlic. Season with salt and pepper. Separate the chicken meat from the bones and add to the sauce. Serve coq au vin with a green salad and baguette.

## TIP !!

It is worthwhile using a good-quality red wine which can then be enjoyed with the meal.

# Saté kebabs

Preparation time approx. 35 minutes | plus marinating time approx. 1 hour | ready in approx. 1 hour 35 minutes
Moderate | per portion approx. 210 kcal/ 880 kJ, 31 g P, 7 g F, 5 g CH

## SERVES 4

1 piece of ginger root
  (approx. 3 cm)
1 garlic clove
125 ml unsweetened coconut
  milk
1 tbsp brown sugar
1 tsp turmeric powder
1 tsp cumin
3 tbsp light soy sauce
salt
black pepper
bunch coriander
500 g chicken breast fillets

**1** Peel the ginger, slice thinly to begin with, then cut into small cubes. Peel and very finely chop the garlic. Pour the coconut milk into a bowl with the ginger, brown sugar, turmeric, cumin and soy sauce. Mix well, then season with salt and pepper. Wash the coriander and pat dry on kitchen towel. Tear the leaves off the stems and chop very finely with a large kitchen knife before adding to the coconut milk.

**2** Rinse the chicken breasts in cold water, pat dry and cut into thin slices. Spear the chicken slices onto kebab skewers, pushing the meat along the skewer in such a way that it forms waves. Pour the marinade over the meat. Cover and stand in a cool place for at least 1–2 hours, turning occasionally and brushing with marinade.

**3** Once the meat has marinated thoroughly, remove the saté skewers from the marinade, drain briefly and grill under an electric grill for 2–3 minutes on each side. This dish can also be prepared in the oven. Pre-heat the grill as indicated in your oven manual and cook the kebabs on a metal rack on the top shelf. Turn over after 2–3 minutes. Serve the kebabs with an Asian-style sauce, e.g. peanut sauce.

**TIP!!**

Serve with basmati rice to turn this into a main meal.

# Duck breast with pomegranate sauce

Preparation time **approx. 40 minutes** | plus frying time **approx. 12 minutes** | ready in **approx. 50 minutes**
Moderate | per portion approx. 620 kcal/2604 kJ, 29 g P, 35 g F, 47 g CH

## SERVES 4

2 duck breast fillets
4 shallots
3 tbsp oil
salt
pepper
50 g almonds, chopped
200 ml chicken stock
200 ml pomegranate syrup
1 pomegranate

**1** Wash the duck breasts, pat dry and make criss-cross cuts in the skin. Peel and slice the shallots into rings.

**2** Heat 2 tablespoons of oil and brown the duck breasts over a high heat, skins facing down, for 6 minutes. Season with salt and pepper, turn and fry on the other side for another 6 minutes over a reduced heat. Remove the duck breasts from the frying pan, wrap in aluminium foil and leave to rest in a warm oven heated to approx. 50 °C for 10 minutes.

**3** Heat the remaining oil with the duck juices left in the frying pan, then sweat the shallots until translucent. Add the almonds, then pour in the chicken stock. Stir in the pomegranate syrup and cook for a while until the sauce is reduced.

**4** Slice the pomegranate in half and extract the seeds. Season the sauce with salt and pepper to taste, then stir in the pomegranate seeds. Remove the duck breast fillets from the oven, cut into slices and serve with the pomegranate sauce. Rice or bread make good companions to this dish.

## TIP !!

To extract the seeds from a pomegranate: fill a large bowl with water. Cut open the pomegranate, then break into small chunks. You will find that the seeds practically fall out of their own accord or can be easily removed by hand. They will then sink to the bottom of the bowl.

# Saltimbocca alla romana

Preparation time approx. 30 minutes
Moderate | per portion approx. 360 kcal/1512 kJ, 44 g P, 14 g F, 1 g CH

## SERVES 4

4 large, thinly sliced veal
  escalopes (180 g each)
black pepper, freshly ground
12 wafer-thin slices of raw ham
12 sage leaves
3 tbsp butter
1 tbsp ice-cold butter, flaked
salt
125 ml dry white wine

**1** Wash the veal escalopes, pat dry and divide each one into three equal pieces. Beat the meat to make it thinner, then season lightly with pepper. Lay a slice of ham and a sage leaf flat on top of each piece of escalope and thread a wooden cocktail stick through the surface to keep the ham and sage in place.

**2** Melt 3 tablespoons of butter in a frying pan. Brown the meat for approx. 2–3 minutes on both sides. Season lightly with salt, and another sprinkling of pepper, then remove from the pan. Cover and keep warm in the oven at about 50 °C.

**3** Mix the wine with the cooking juices in the frying pan and bring to a rapid boil for about 2 minutes. Whisk the ice-cold butter into the sauce. Season to taste and return the schnitzels to sit in the sauce for a few more minutes. Serve with a fresh, green salad and pasta or bread.

## TIP!!

Saltimbocca alla romana is an absolute classic of Roman cuisine. Literally translated from Italian, it means "jump in the mouth" – and it's true: these little schnitzels are so delicious that people would be waiting with wide-open mouths to catch them!

# Involtini

Preparation time **approx. 20 minutes** | plus cooking time **approx. 20 minutes** | ready in **approx. 40 minutes**
Moderate | per portion **approx. 353 kcal/1482 kJ, 38 g P, 16 g F, 6 g CH**

## SERVES 4

8 small veal escalopes
salt
pepper
50 g air-dried ham
100 g chicken livers, chopped
1 tbsp each parsley and thyme,
  both freshly chopped
1 garlic clove
3 tbsp freshly grated Parmesan
3 tbsp flour
5 tbsp butter
200 ml dry white wine

**1** Beat the veal escalopes to flatten them, then season with salt and pepper. Finely dice the ham and mix with the chopped chicken liver and herbs. Peel and chop the garlic clove, then stir the grated Parmesan into the ham and liver mixture.

**2** Spread this mixture over the escalopes, then roll them up and secure with a cocktail stick. Coat the veal rolls in flour. Heat the butter in a frying pan and brown the involtini on all sides for about 3 minutes. Add the white wine and cook all the ingredients for about 20 minutes. Season again to taste with salt and pepper.

## TIP!!

It is always better to use freshly grated Parmesan – the ready-grated version sold in packets simply cannot compete!

**Simply elegant**

# Scallops wrapped in bacon

Preparation time **approx. 25 minutes**

Quick and easy | per portion approx. 223 kcal/936 kJ, 27 g P, 6 g F, 12 g CH

## SERVES 4

24 fresh scallops in their shells
24 thin slices of bacon
cayenne pepper
1 unwaxed lemon

**1** Using a sharp knife, carefully prise the white scallop meat from its shell without damaging it. Remove the roe.

**2** Wrap each scallop firmly in a slice of bacon. Spear 3 scallop and bacon parcels on each metal skewer.

**3** Grill the scallop kebabs under a pre-heated grill for about 4 minutes. Sprinkle with cayenne pepper and serve with wedges of lemon. Serve with freshly baked garlic bread and grilled cherry tomatoes.

*A delicious and elegant appetiser*

# King prawns in tomato sauce

Preparation time **approx. 20 minutes** | plus cooking time **approx. 20 minutes** | ready in **approx. 40 minutes**
Quick and easy | per portion **approx. 345 kcal/1449 kJ, 51 g P, 9 g F, 5 g CH**

## SERVES 4

1 onion
1 garlic clove
4 tbsp olive oil
½ small chilli pepper
2 bay leaves
100 q tomato purée (tinned)
1 kg king prawns, peeled and
  deveined
200 ml white wine
2 tbsp freshly chopped parsley

**1** Peel and chop the onion and garlic clove. Heat the olive oil in a frying pan. Sweat the onion and garlic in the hot oil until translucent. De-seed and chop the chilli pepper, then add to the onions along with the bay leaves. Add the tomato purée and simmer all the ingredients together for about 10 minutes.

**2** Wash the king prawns, pat dry, then add to the sauce and season with salt. Pour in the white wine, then cover and simmer for about 10 minutes. Do not overcook otherwise the king prawns will become tough. Serve sprinkled with chopped parsley and an accompaniment of white bread.

# Garlic king prawns

Preparation time approx. 20 minutes

Quick and easy | per portion approx. 168 kcal/706 kJ, 13 g P, 11 g F, 4 g CH

## SERVES 4

2 garlic cloves
1 red chilli pepper
6 tbsp olive oil
24 king prawns, peeled and
    deveined
salt
pepper
4 tbsp flour

**1** Peel the garlic cloves, clean and finely chop the chilli pepper. Heat the olive oil in a frying pan, then add the garlic and chilli and fry for 3 minutes until the aromas begin to be released. Remove from the pan.

**2** Wash the king prawns and pat dry. Season with salt and pepper, then coat in flour and brown in the flavoured oil for about 2 minutes on all sides. Serve hot with fresh bread and salad.

# Clam curry with aubergines

Preparation time approx. 35 minutes
Moderate | per portion approx. 507 kcal/2123 kJ, 36 g P, 28 g F, 33 g CH

## SERVES 4

2 kg clams, in their shells
8 garlic cloves
12 small round Thai aubergines,
   or 4 European aubergines
   instead
10 kaffir lime leaves, or else
   5 stems of Thai basil, frozen
6 tbsp oil
2 tbsp yellow curry paste
8 tbsp fish sauce
4 tbsp light soy sauce
4 tsp sugar

**1** Wash the clams thoroughly, discarding any which have opened. Peel and finely dice the garlic. Trim and wash the aubergines, then dice into cubes approx. 2 cm square.

**2** Wash the lime leaves, pat dry, cut out the central rib and slice the leaves into fine strips. Wash the Thai basil, shake dry and tear off the leaves.

**3** Heat the oil in a wok or saucepan, then fry the garlic for approx. 2 minutes until golden. Stir in the curry paste and fry briefly. Tip in the clams, followed by the rest of the ingredients, stirring constantly.

**4** Cook the curry for 5–8 minutes. Once the clams have opened up, dish them out into pre-warmed bowls, discarding any shells which have failed to open.

## TIP!!

Any clams which have opened before being cooked must be removed and discarded as they will have gone bad. The same applies to any shells which fail to open during cooking: they will have gone off and must be discarded.

# Sautéd salmon on asparagus

Preparation time approx. 40 minutes
Moderate | per portion approx. 432 kcal/1814 kJ, 43 g P, 24 g F, 9 g CH

## SERVES 4

600 g salmon fillet
3 garlic cloves
bunch flat-leaf parsley
1 unwaxed lime
750 g white asparagus
750 g green asparagus
80 g Parmesan
salt
3 tbsp olive oil
20 g pine kernels
white pepper

**1** Wash the salmon fillet, pat dry, then cut into 4. Peel and slice the garlic. Wash the parsley, pat dry, then finely chop. Wash, dry and slice the lime.

**2** Wash and peel the white asparagus. Wash the green asparagus and peel the lower third of the spears. Finely grate the Parmesan. Cook the white asparagus in lightly salted boiling water for 12–15 minutes. After 5–8 minues, add the green asparagus to the saucepan.

**3** Meanwhile, heat the olive oil and sauté the salmon on both sides for about 5 minutes. After 4 minutes, add the sliced lime, garlic and pine kernels and brown briefly. Season with parsley, salt and pepper.

**4** Arrange the asparagus on the plates. Place each salmon fillet on a bed of asparagus and serve sprinkled with Parmesan. Serve with rice or baguette.

Great treat during asparagus season

# Fish Curry with Coriander and yoghurt

Preparation time **approx. 25 minutes** | plus cooking time **approx. 10 minutes** | ready in **approx. 35 minutes**
Moderate | per portion **approx. 260 kcal/1092 kJ, 40 g P, 6 g F, 8 g CH**

## SERVES 4

750 g halibut fillet
juice of 1 lemon
2 onions
1 garlic clove
1 tbsp butter
½ bunch freshly chopped
   coriander
1 tsp turmeric
2 tsp curry
1 tbsp coconut milk
6 tomatoes
150 g yoghurt
salt
pepper

**1** Wash the fish fillet, pat dry and cut into bite-sized pieces. Drizzle with lemon juice.

**2** Peel and finely chop the onions and garlic clove. Heat the butter in a saucepan, then fry the onions and garlic until translucent. Add the coriander, spices and coconut milk to the pan and cook for another 3 minutes.

**3** Wash and dry the tomatoes, remove the stalks and cores, then cut in half. Add to the saucepan. Cook all the ingredients for another 5 minutes. Stir in the yoghurt, and heat, but do not allow to boil otherwise it will curdle.

**4** Add the fish chunks to the sauce, cover and cook over a low heat for about 10 minutes. Season with salt and pepper. Serve with rice.

## TIP!!

Any type of firm white fish, e.g. tilapia or redfish, can be used instead of halibut.

# Index A–Z

# Index according to food type

## ABBREVIATIONS

tbsp = tablespoon
g = gram
kcal = kilocalorie
kg = kilogram
kJ = kilojoule
l = litre
ml = millilitre
tsp = teaspoon

## COMMON KITCHEN MEASUREMENTS

1 teaspoon (tsp) = 5 ml
1 tablespoon (tbsp) = 15 ml
1 cup = 120 ml
1 (US) cup = 240 ml
1 soup bowl = 250 ml
1 schnapps glass = 20 ml = 2 cl
1 water glass = 200 ml
1 cup semolina = 96 g
1 cup oat flakes = 72 g
1 cup flour = 96 g
1 cup rice = 96 g
1 cup sugar = 100 g

## PICTURE CREDITS